Gentle. Loving. This tender book asks us to listen to our pain, lean into our discomfort, and trust that we can be lifted back on our feet by God and each other.

> **Kate C. Bowler,** *New York Times* bestselling
> author of *No Cure for Being Human*

There are so many ways you can lose the only life you know how to live. When that happens—as it will for all of us sooner or later—the number of people willing to walk through it with us can fall into the low single digits. With this book, Shauna Niequist becomes one you can count on, no matter what. She won't lie to you about anything. She won't offer you a spiritual bypass. Instead, she will keep reminding you that what you don't know about where you're going is what oils the hinge to new life.

> **Barbara Brown Taylor,** author of
> *Learning to Walk in the Dark*

This book is a masterpiece. It is a journey and an invitation and a joy and a heartbreak and all the things you need to read to be reminded that hope can still be found.

> **Annie F. Downs,** *New York Times* bestselling
> author of *That Sounds Fun*

A seminary professor of mine once asked our class to ponder the question, "What is the good life?" for an entire hour-long period. I never found the perfect answer to that question, but this book may be the closest I've come. Shauna Niequist reminds us that the abundant life isn't gained by striving or winning, but by mustering enough courage to forge ahead when our lives fall apart. She offers us the tools we need to build resistance in an age of trauma and to manage the perils of human existence in a world that is changing at warp speed. When others may preach or lecture, Shauna wonders and imagines. *I Guess I Haven't Learned That Yet* is a 240-page invitation into a life where change is anticipated, evolution is embraced, and *learning* is just another word for *living*. If that's not the good life, then I don't know what is.

> **Jonathan Merritt,** contributing writer for *The Atlantic*
> and author of *Learning to Speak God from Scratch*

i guess
i haven't
learned
that yet

Other Books by Shauna Niequist

Cold Tangerines

Bittersweet

Bread & Wine

Savor

Present Over Perfect

i guess i haven't learned that yet

DISCOVERING NEW WAYS OF LIVING WHEN THE OLD WAYS STOP WORKING

shauna niequist

New York Times bestselling author of *PRESENT OVER PERFECT*

ZONDERVAN BOOKS

ZONDERVAN BOOKS

I Guess I Haven't Learned That Yet
Copyright © 2022 by Shauna Niequist

Requests for information should be addressed to:
Zondervan, *3900 Sparks Dr. SE, Grand Rapids, Michigan 49546*

Zondervan titles may be purchased in bulk for educational, business, fundraising, or sales promotional use. For information, please email SpecialMarkets@Zondervan.com.

ISBN 978-0-310-35559-5 (international trade paper edition)
ISBN 978-0-310-35558-8 (audio)

Library of Congress Cataloging-in-Publication Data

Names: Niequist, Shauna, author.
Title: I guess I haven't learned that yet : discovering new ways of living when the old ways stop working / Shauna Niequist.
Description: Grand Rapids : Zondervan, 2022. | Summary: "New York Times bestselling author Shauna Niequist writes about unexpected loss, change, faith, midlife, and a move to New York City with her signature depth and vulnerability. In this book, she invites us to practice curiosity and self-compassion, to become beginners again, and to rediscover resilience and courage in our own seasons of change"— Provided by publisher.
Identifiers: LCCN 2021047936 (print) | LCCN 2021047937 (ebook) | ISBN 9780310355564 (hardcover) | ISBN 9780310355571 (ebook)
Subjects: LCSH: Niequist, Shauna. | Christian life. | Christian biography.
Classification: LCC BR1725.N525 A3 2022 (print) | LCC BR1725.N525 (ebook) | DDC 277.308/3092 [B]—dc23/eng/20211221
LC record available at https://lccn.loc.gov/2021047936
LC ebook record available at https://lccn.loc.gov/2021047937

Author is represented by The Christopher Ferebee Agency, www.christopherferebee.com.

Cover design: Lindy Martin / Faceout Studio
Cover illustration: h.yegho / Shutterstock
Interior design: Kait Lamphere

Printed in the United States of America

22 23 24 25 26 27 28 29 30 31 /LSC/ 14 13 12 11 10 9 8 7 6 5 4 3 2 1

For General Theological Seminary,
Good Shepherd New York,
and the city of New York
for welcoming me home
to myself

Contents

PART 5: *Still Yes*

Catching the Light: An Introduction

I'm sitting at my desk, looking out at the Close—that's what they call the green space in the center of the seminary where we live. Our apartment is on the third floor, our bedroom windows face south, and I've wedged a tiny child-sized desk between our bed and the bookcases, because catching the light is always my priority.

This morning, Aaron and Henry took the subway to Henry's first morning of high school orientation. Henry is tall, broad-shouldered, handsome. He's funny and kind and wears dress pants and has fabulously long, shaggy hair that he's forever sweeping out of his eyes. The week I was offered a contract to write my first book was the same week I found out I was pregnant with him, and this morning I'm feeling the full circle of this—these books and stories, the writer I have become inextricably entwined with the mother I became when Henry was born.

This book you're holding is one I've been writing and rewriting for years, and as much as I've struggled with it, the struggle has healed me, helped me, and forced me to make sense of my story and our world—as much as anyone can. Being a writer means being committed to paying attention, to walking through the world as a noticer. It means finding language for the seemingly unspeakable, using words to bridge the divides between us, telling stories that narrate and renarrate who we are in the world and what the world means to us.

One of the challenges of this book was defining the edges. Can it be about this too, and also this? How far can it stretch before it's just a junk drawer? But looking back, I've pushed the edges in this way in every book I've written—a book about cooking is also about babies and friendship and prayer; a book about celebration is also about losing your job and forgiveness and Paris. Because that's how life is—interconnected and multifaceted. We carry around our whole selves—our past and our parents, our loves and our limitations, our dreams and our grocery lists and our wounds. That's how it always is.

It may seem chaotic or like a disparate mishmash of topics and themes, as I try to write a book that encompasses faith and curiosity, compassion and self-compassion, learning to let go and learning to be a beginner again, midlife and menopause and moving. But this is how I think the world works, how our minds and spirits and conversations work—or at least how mine do.

When I walk with a friend or call my mother, or when we meet our neighbors in the courtyard for a glass of wine, we talk about God and *The Crown* and what's the name of that French place down on Hudson? We talk about how our kids are doing and *Ted Lasso* and biscuits and hard conversations with family and doctor's appointments and shoes. We talk about politics and our work and where to get good dumplings and why no one's sleeping well these days and how much we miss things like dance floors and weddings and reasons to dress up.

As I'm writing this, we are still in the midst of a global pandemic. We know that the world has been and is being altered—that much is clear. But so much, too, is unclear—altered how?

At the very least, it seems that two core myths are being handily dismantled in the face of this pandemic: first, the myth of control, and second, the myth of independence. There are things that can run through our lives, ravaging them, leaving them unrecognizable, and there's nothing we can do to prevent them—like a virus. And our choices affect one another every day, all the time. Control and independence have been exposed, at this point, for the mirages that they are, pipe dreams, vestiges of another world.

So what do we do? We pay attention. We accept the world as it is, not as we wish it was. We practice—we build rhythms of health and faith and grounding, ways of living that allow our best selves to emerge and our worst selves to recede as often as possible. We help each other. And we discipline ourselves to stay on the lookout for signs of hope, for sacred moments and divine fingerprints even in a desolate and quiet landscape—especially in this desolate and quiet landscape.

This is in no way a comprehensive overview of spiritual practices—or a comprehensive anything, really. I'm a forty-something mother of two, a Midwesterner living in Manhattan. I'm sometimes tired and sometimes afraid, sometimes hopeful and sometimes despairing. I would not call myself an expert in almost anything, except possibly Kennedy trivia and last-minute dinner parties. I am certainly not an expert on spiritual life.

But I am, just as you are, living in a world that feels dry as a desert some days, like the very spirit has been leached away, leaving only bone and outrage. And I'm longing for life, living water, nourishment, and direction. I want to live a faithful, meaningful life. I want to feel God's presence, bring about his kingdom, tell his story in every way I know how. And these are, quite simply, the things I've learned along the way as I travel the path of faith.

This is not a to-do list. This is not a prescription for success or a road map to spiritual perfection. This is a love letter, a handful of treasures, a lifeline, a hand reaching out in the darkness and offering hope and respite. I am old enough to have learned a few things that sustain us when the night is long, the sky dark, the journey rough, and I'm offering them to you. My prayer is that they will be useful and helpful—for your soul and spirit, for your breath and body—on the journey home.

This is the book I wish someone had written for me when I was in a season of near-constant untethering and unbelonging, wandering and fumbling, and ultimately discovering a million beautiful surprises after a couple of very dark years. There are seasons for tidy prose, and this is decidedly not one of them. This is everything I know—wild and messy, accompaniments for the hardest stretches of the journey.

This is not about what I've been through; this is about what remains, in all our lives, when the deals and agreements and myths and illusions have been washed away by pain and loss and years. This is about a search for grounding when nothing feels stable, the yearning for peace in a raging storm.

It's about curiosity and compassion, and it's about spiritual practices to weather the rough passages, but at the center it's about leaving behind what needs to be left behind, accepting the spirit of the age. It's about learning to stand alone, leaving behind the identities you believed you could never live without.

part one

Gravity of Love

one

I Guess I Haven't Learned That Yet

My husband, Aaron, and I and our boys, Henry and Mac, are lifelong Midwesterners, but three years ago we moved to Manhattan.

We made the move from a house in the suburbs of Chicago to an 825-square-foot apartment on the third floor of a beautiful neo-Gothic redbrick building in the Chelsea neighborhood of New York City. A few days later, the kids started school—Mac at a primary school just a block away, and Henry at a middle school down in the West Village. These were great schools, and our kids had come from great schools, but inevitably there were gaps—things that our boys hadn't yet covered in their old schools, things that felt unfamiliar or frustrating.

About six weeks after we moved, in an extremely low-budget decorating move, I wrote one sentence on a piece of printer paper and taped it to our living room wall with bright blue painter's tape: *I guess I haven't learned that yet.*

I put it on our wall because it seemed like our boys were coming home from their new schools every day with the same question: *Why do they know this and I don't?* They kept running into places where the curricula from their old schools and their

7

new schools didn't quite match up. At Henry's old school he took French, but at his new school Spanish is mandatory. At Mac's old school they learned guitar, but at this new school everyone takes piano.

The boys were doing great, but they had a lot of questions, and what I realized was that there were deeper questions under their questions—they were asking about piano and recess and buses and lockers, but what they were really asking was, *Have I failed? Have I fallen behind? Am I dumb?*

I said, Oh my darlings, you're not dumb—you're new. We're all new. And we're not failing. But we're learning, and it's exhausting and humbling and fun and hard. You know how my success rate on the subway is around fifty–fifty? And you know how I always have to text Dad to meet me on Ninth Avenue because I bought too many groceries and can't carry them all the way home, because I'm used to having an SUV, and now all I have are my arms?

I guess I haven't learned that yet. I wrote that sentence because I wanted us to have a common language for what it means to be a learner, a beginner, to be curious and make mistakes and get back up. To ask questions and figure it out as we go.

I told the boys that each of us was going to say that phrase every single day about something, and that it was a good thing, not a bad thing. Not knowing something already doesn't make you bad or dumb; it doesn't mean you failed. Not knowing something doesn't mean you're falling behind or fundamentally flawed. It just means there's more to learn.

We used that phrase over and over, intentionally, as a way of reminding ourselves that this is part of moving, part of being a rookie again. And as the weeks and months passed, I felt something shifting inside me. Instead of this beginner label being a balm over a wound, a corrective measure against shame or blame, I began to like it, to try it on and wear it around, not just when I got off at the wrong subway stop, but as often as I could. And I started liking how it felt to be a beginner in more than just city living. It's changing my writing, my marriage, my parenting. It's bringing curiosity and freedom and peace.

Because without realizing it, I had been wearing an expert hat for a long time—as a parent, as a writer, as someone who had lived in her hometown for a long time. I was the expert. The answer person. But I don't have all the answers anymore. I have to ask for help or direction every single day, and you know what? I like it.

We're talking about curiosity and freedom, but under those things, what we're talking about is self-compassion—treating yourself with the same care and kindness you'd show to someone you love.

This does not come naturally to me. I have a long history of saying things to myself—about my body, about my feelings, about my failures—that I would never say to another living human.

Self-compassion is letting yourself off the hook, letting yourself be human and flawed and also amazing. It's giving yourself credit for showing up instead of beating yourself up for taking so long to get there.

A friend of mine is a researcher and therapist, and we were talking about self-compassion recently. He reminded me that the research on this topic is overwhelmingly clear—the energy of self-compassion fuels so much more lasting change in our lives than shame or guilt or self-loathing ever could. We find the courage to change when we feel loved. It unlocks our ability to move forward and grow.

The best way to start practicing self-compassion is to tap into the kindness you show other people. So many of us are voices of love for the other people in our lives, and it's when we learn to speak with that same voice of love to ourselves that we're able to make meaningful change. Self-compassion is learning to say, *I guess I haven't learned that yet.*

Earlier this spring, I was on the phone with my mom. Probably I was crying—please tell me I'm not the only one who still starts to cry the second she hears her mom's concerned voice on the phone. My mom said, "Hey, I wanted to tell you something. I've been going through my old journals, and it made me think of you. When I was in my midforties, I wrote this line: 'Every single thing that used to work has just stopped working, all at the same time.'"

"Whoa," I said. "I know," she replied. That was exactly what I had been saying—or a teary, more dramatic version of it—for months.

Since my fortieth birthday, almost every part and pattern of my life has shifted in a major way. Some of those changes have been intentional; many of them have been changes I didn't choose. There have been stretches in the last few years when I've been surprised I could still recognize my own face in the mirror, my life having been so profoundly altered in so many ways.

My eyes see the world in ways I didn't before—less naivete, more compassion, more awareness of the suffering many people have been carrying for years, even when I was unaware.

I've moved from being the mother of little boys—all snuggles and wiggles—to parenting middle and high school boys, other animals entirely. I've weathered a stretch of heartbreak and grief deeper and darker and more volatile than anything I'd ever experienced before. I've struggled with my health, struggled in my body, struggled to make sense of and find solutions for chronic pain and insomnia. I've ended some friendships, which is so hard. I've had some end for me, and that's even harder. I've learned to live in a smaller, quieter world, and I've been surprised at how much I like it.

After a lifetime in the suburbs and small towns, I'm a city dweller now, and a delighted one. Even after a few years, I'm still enchanted by New York, still enamored with its beauty and quirks and challenges and gifts. I have a little cart for my groceries, a decent grasp of the subway system, and strong feelings about the best pizza in the city.

There are things that remain, through lines I've held to like lifelines in this season of compounded change and chaos. Our marriage, my faith, my work as a writer, and my love for the table remain constant, although even those things have been refined—altered as a result of all the other altering.

That's how it works. The changes connect and cascade, and the only way through it, it seems to me, is with curiosity and self-compassion, one in each hand, the tools for the journey. I'm not a natural at either one, although I'm learning to practice both with increasing regularity. There's so much I don't know, so much I've gotten wrong, so much I still want to learn and experience and understand as life unfolds. I keep moving forward, keep putting one foot in front of the other, holding tightly to the greatest gifts I've been given in recent years— curiosity and self-compassion. Apply as needed, over and over and over.

two

Shoulders Down, Heart Open

I tend to scrunch my shoulders up around my ears more often than not. I'm doing it as I write—such a bad habit—and once again I have to consciously force myself to roll my shoulders back and down, to propel my chest open by filling my lungs, to spread my shoulders wide and low.

A woman named Blue gave me a massage once, and afterward I asked her if there was anything unusual about my muscles and bones, anything she noticed that I should pay special attention to. She answered right away and told me what every massage therapist, chiropractor, and doctor I've ever asked has told me: Your shoulders are a problem. Lots of people have problems with their shoulders, but you have bad problems.

I asked her about a solution, and she said less time in front of a screen, more stretching. And then she asked, "Do you want to hear my theory? I mean, I made it up, but it makes sense to me. When you lift your shoulders all the way up, what happens? Like, what is your body trying to do when you do that? Seems to me it's trying to cover your ears and cover your heart at the same time. And that makes me wonder. What is it that you don't want to hear? What is it that you don't want to feel inside your heart?

"Here's another thing," she said. "And again, this is just what I see, what I figure—when you were really young, did someone ever make you feel like you should be smaller than you were, or bigger than you were?"

There were so many things I didn't want my heart to feel. There were so many things I didn't want my ears to hear. And all my life, I've tried to be smaller, smaller, smaller. I was still reeling from a terrible season of leaving home and leaving a church that felt more like a home than any actual home I'd ever lived in. I was grieving the loss of relationships, the loss of the world as I knew it, and the pain was emotional, of course, but deeply physical too.

The chronic physical pain that I asked Blue about was ratcheting up in intensity with each passing month—the muscles along the tops of my shoulders felt like bone or rock, and by the end of the day, I'd alternate between too much Advil and too much wine, trying to deaden the pain. I was going on year three or four of unexplained stomach pain and IBS-like symptoms that came and went, and after being a champion sleeper for most of my life, I was cycling through stretches of insomnia that were absolutely crazymaking.

It was physical and emotional both, certainly, but I wasn't having any luck finding solutions on either side—not conventional medicine, not chiropractic care, not dietary changes. For a while I was carrying around a pillbox that looked more like a tackle box, filled to the brim with every manner of natural supplement and enzyme. They didn't help. During an extreme IBS flare-up, I spent one trip to New York extremely attached to an app that maps every public bathroom across the city. I told a friend that my body had lost its mind, and I couldn't find anything that helped—or at least anything that helped for long.

I kept coming back to Blue's words, and when I did, I practiced rolling my shoulders down, opening my heart, over and over. I began asking questions I wasn't at all sure I wanted the answers to.

There wasn't a solution exactly, but more like a befriending. I started listening to the pain instead of trying to cover over it. A friend recommended the work of Dr. Sarno, and Aaron came home one afternoon to find me lying on the living room rug, staring at the ceiling. "You okay?" he asked tentatively. I stayed on the floor but told him about Dr. Sarno's findings, that some of us who experience chronic physical pain need to learn to feel our unfeelable feelings and think our unthinkable thoughts.

Dr. Sarno's work features story after story of people who have suffered in terrible ways for years, unable to work or parent or live the lives they want because of crippling pain, and then when they learn to welcome those thoughts and those feelings, the pain finally begins to recede. It reminded me of Blue's words to me: *What is it that you don't want to hear? What is it that you don't want to feel inside your heart?*

A million things, at least. I needed to change my life, but I didn't want to. The life I'd imagined for our family and our future no longer existed. That was a lot to feel, certainly, a lot to open one's heart to, and so it was much easier, for a while at least, to keep my shoulders up, my muscles brittle like bones.

I started to welcome it all, feel it all. Some days I couldn't, but most days I tried, and the practice is changing me, the questions are changing me, the feelings and thoughts I've tried not to feel for so long are changing me from the inside out, opening a heart that's been fighting to keep itself safely closed for a long time.

three

Finding a New Way

Aaron and I lived in a hometown with a serious number of roots, a subterranean tangle of generations and relationships. We grew up in neighboring suburbs—his high school played ours in sports, and we had a million mutual friends. His family had lived on the same property since the 1940s—a piece of land that his grandpa bought when that area was still rural, not yet suburban. His dad and uncles are chiropractors at the same clinic his grandpa started in the fifties.

My parents started a church the year I was born, and for nine years before we moved to New York, Aaron and I lived within walking distance of it. Our kids were in the school district I was raised in, and their Little League coaches were guys I went to high school with.

Every single day, I saw cousins and friends from high school and neighbors and people from church I'd known all my life. Familiarity, history, roots driven down so deep it was like one of those underground parking garages that corkscrews down so many stories you think you must be nearing the earth's actual core.

And I loved it. I loved that web of relationships, that sense of being known and taken care of. Of being in the center of an impenetrable circle of safety and history. I reveled in it.

Aaron had joined the world I lived in, but it wasn't the world he wanted. It was my family, my church, my town, my dream. And I gave him a lovely little corner. But he didn't want it—not the corner, not the life. He never did. He wanted the two of us to be a separate unit, explorers, adventurers, out on our own, connecting occasionally but warmly with that old world.

Aaron had always been close to his family, and those relationships were important to him, but increasingly the tight circling of our church and my family and the expectations and requirements of that way of living chafed him.

His faith was shifting, and so was mine—but for better or worse, my family loyalty was a higher priority to me than finding a church that matched my evolving spiritual perspective, and also, I wasn't the one who worked there. I traveled a lot and had all the creative freedom and autonomy in the world—meanwhile, Aaron was working at my family's church, feeling distinctly less creative freedom and autonomy. It's all so clear now in ways it should have been then—one of the things I regret most acutely is my habit of seeing only what I wanted to see.

I was blinded by what I wanted—the church and our little family and my extended family to find its center point at my kitchen counter three nights a week. I wanted to wrap our life in layers and layers of familiarity and cozy blankets, and there was only one problem with that: it was not in any way the life Aaron wanted.

When he left his job at our family's church, Aaron wanted to visit new churches. This was not an unreasonable request in general, except that it tapped into one million feelings of family loyalty.

Looking back, I see it, of course. He wanted freedom and autonomy so badly, and I kept trying to sell him on things he fundamentally didn't want. Because I had no desire for that kind of freedom and autonomy and was pretty afraid of it, if I'm honest.

For one of the first times in our married life, it felt like the lives we wanted weren't just different, but mutually exclusive. Like any two people who feel like what they're longing for doesn't matter to the other person, we both got louder and more afraid. We sometimes yelled and sometimes cried.

We sometimes flew to other cities, other churches. We sometimes felt like Goldilocks, looking for a new life, but we definitely weren't finding "just right"—was it because I really wasn't as open as I promised I was? Entirely possible. Or was it something else? Something calling us or keeping us in our hometown? I hoped so. It felt like we knocked on a thousand doors that didn't open, and in the meantime, our kids were thriving in good schools, benefiting from lots of time with all four grandparents and loads of aunts and uncles and cousins. That was enough to stay, right?

We got into complicated trades: You can decide where we go to church if we can keep the kids in their schools. We can try to get Cubs season tickets. I don't need that farmhouse after all—just don't ask me to move to this city or that town. No, we don't have to do every vacation with extended family. It wasn't great, but we inched back toward each other and out of the terrible all-or-nothing, what-I-want-or-what-you-want tug-of-war.

We cobbled together a plan to find a new way to live in the same town, separate from my family's church. We'd maybe move that summer, but within the same school district. Maybe we were finding a new way.

four

On Crying in Church

On a Sunday morning in February, in a small white-steepled church, the oldest in our hometown, a brilliant African American preacher named Zina gave a sermon that unraveled something inside me, pulled back the curtain on what I'd been trying so hard to hide, even from myself—maybe especially from myself.

She talked about loss and change and suffering and how we don't yet know the end or the meaning or the moral of the story, the tidy conclusion. But we keep going in the middle, the long, difficult middle, knowing we'll know later. She talked about Joseph and his brothers and how you just don't know the whole story when you're in the middle of it.

We were sitting in Zina's church because we no longer attended the church my family started. The process of leaving was painful, and those early visits to new churches were terrible. I cried in the car and sometimes in the pews. I was thankful for the hospitality of church members, but I never knew what to say. *No, we're not new in town. No, this isn't the first time we've ever been to church. Yes, you can take my picture to show your daughter.*

Aaron and I and our family were in a wilderness of sorts, having left behind something that had been stable and stabilizing for many years and now staring at a blank space where the future used to be. I was feeling lonely, disconnected from the tradition that raised me, the songs that were my soundtrack, the rhythms that felt more familiar to me than my own hands.

We're living in a time of such deep loneliness, vitriol, disillusionment. So many of us are breaking away from the things that used to tether us, whether that's a political party, a church, a marriage, a denomination, a family. Many of our treasured connections have been severed in this season as the middle ground evaporates and the cry of us versus them becomes deafening.

A dear friend wishes she knew another married couple who disagrees about politics as deeply and painfully as she and her husband do. Another friend left her church because her beliefs have shifted and there is no room for that shift at her church. Another friend feels torn between his marriage and his family of origin, blamed for not being there enough in either relationship.

The shifts feel tectonic right now. Maybe they always do, in every generation. But this is the first time in my lifetime that so many of us are distrustful of the systems that have held us stable for so long. And when we disconnect from those systems, we find ourselves profoundly lonely.

I still believe in God—in his goodness especially. In the centrality of forgiveness, confession, prayer. I believe he is present in our lives, that he offers comfort and wisdom, that the way of Christ is the best possible way to live. I still believe in religion as a meaningful way to gather and organize our lives, although I don't believe it's a stand-in for emotional health or self-awareness or character, and I don't believe a devoutly religious person is necessarily any of those other important things.

I've shed many illusions. But I am still deeply devout, possibly more than ever. Christ has not failed me. There is no shield against suffering. But there is comfort. And there is presence. And there is healing.

The world is changing faster than we can keep track of it. It's exhausting and scary, and it's tempting to check out, numb out, escape into whatever we can. But our kids need guidance. Our friends and neighbors need support. We have to do this together.

You may, like me, find yourself in midlife—or maybe you're twenty or sixty or eighty—and all of a sudden, the life you planned is gone. And the world you thought you lived in is gone. And the assumptions and beliefs that carried you through up to this moment have dumped you unceremoniously into a foreign land. You don't speak the language. You don't know anyone.

But the sun keeps coming up every morning, to your surprise. Life is still happening, here on the other side, here on the distant planet you live on now. And you realize that your old life is gone. And also you notice you're still alive, very much so. You're still raising children—beautiful, silly children who need you to make their toast and sign their forms and tuck them in at night, even here in this other universe.

Everything has changed and also you still have work to do and dirty dishes in the sink, and where your future used to be, now there's a blank nothingness and you realize you have to build a new life. You have to paint the canvas of your future, because it used to be such a well-developed, very specific image and now it is blank. This is terrifying. At some point—I promise—it will be a tiny bit exciting, this blankness.

But right now, you might be crying in church the same way I have dozens of times. You're not alone. We never are.

The pain and isolation are very real, and the tears streaming down your face are valuable, sacred, holy. If anyone tries to tell you that walking away from a church you've loved or a tradition you've loved or a community of faith you've loved is an easy thing to do, they're lying to you. For me, it felt surgical. Sometimes it still does.

But also sometimes there are glimpses of hope and healing, there are memories that flood my heart with joy, there is a flutter of hope for the future, not just my future, but all our futures. Things break and then they heal, stronger for the breaking. But it's absolutely okay to cry along the way.

five

She

Just when Aaron and I had made a tentative, fledgling step into a new way of living, in our marriage and in our town, something truly terrible exploded into our lives, and at the center of it were my dad and our church. While it's not my story to tell, it completely shattered me.

I didn't know how to talk about it, and mostly I still don't. There are things in our lives that carve us so deeply, language fails. This one did that to me, for several reasons. One, I didn't understand it at the time, but my own identity—not my public identity but the inner one, the set of beliefs I carry internally about myself in this world—was unhealthily braided together with my dad and our church.

I understood myself almost entirely in the context of their stories and identities, not my own. Again, this is a weird thing to talk about publicly, especially because I had at that time a public identity and voice of my own—I hadn't used my maiden name for nearly twenty years.

But what this crisis revealed was the extent to which my inner architecture was built on the story of our church and the story of my dad. There are all sorts of reasons for that, and certainly it's not uncommon for the children of parents who have notable lives in some way to become absorbed into that narrative or identity.

The architecture of my inner world crumbled. Who was I? What world was I living in now? How could this be reality? How could this be my real life?

As with any trauma, there's that super-weird side-by-side processing where you're a shell, a ghost, where there is a cavern inside you where your heart used to be, where you can't sleep and sometimes can't breathe and can't imagine having to live in this new, terrible world.

You are amazed that people even recognize your face, because you know that what's happening inside you is unrecognizable, that you're so far off the map you can't even imagine there are words or symbols to mark it.

And then also, weirdly, right at the same time, you're going to your son's fifth-grade graduation. You're talking and laughing and unloading the dishwasher. You're going to therapy, reading, writing. You're doing all the things that healthy people do to get through trauma and crisis. You talk about it with your friends. You cry with them.

This crisis launched in me an excavation that has spanned years. Hundreds of thousands of words written, an ocean of tears.

Let me tell you where I've landed—somewhere else entirely, another planet maybe. A place beyond the events, beyond language, altered entirely. This crisis forced something like a transubstantiation—can I say that? Is that sacrilegious?

I took my own self apart, bone by bone. I asked every question, ripped every seam, dismantled every assumption and agreement until it evaporated to dust.

Where did I land? At the bottom of the ocean, somewhere behind Jupiter. I'm a tiny bird on a branch, a silver fish in the cold ocean. I am someone else and something else entirely. The crisis didn't alter me. What came after did.

And here I am—expectations and sweet sentiments burned away, like flesh scraped from bone. I'm flinty and strong and a little weird and a little wild because I traveled all the way down to the elemental part of myself, and what I found there was this: I'm not the first daughter to buy into a story that her existence is wrapped up wholly in her powerful dad. This happens.

It happens even more extensively when that dad is a public person, especially when he has a powerful emotional and spiritual connection to thousands of people. No one says, "Hey, pal, seems like your dad's voice is a little too loud in your ears." Of course it is. It's too loud in all our ears. This is the water we swim in—what water?

All of a sudden, I could see the water. I could see the extent to which I had built the architecture of my life on someone else's identity. Here's a confession: I would have happily lived that way the rest of my life, cocooned by an identity and story that had kept me safe and stable all my life.

Instead, for a while it felt like walking around without skin, utterly vulnerable, untethered in the deepest way. The world felt terrifying, and I felt lost, unmoored, unfamiliar to my own self.

But what I found, there in the darkness, there at the bottom of the cold ocean, there surrounded by the bits and bones of the self I used to be, was another self. She'd been there all along, but until now I never needed her. She was waiting in the wings, and all of a sudden, I needed her desperately. She is my next self, the one I've been waiting to be all along, without even knowing it. Thank God for her.

This is the story of how I found her—or maybe how she found me.

six

Corpse Reviver

Sometimes when people ask why we moved from the suburbs of Chicago to the heart of Manhattan, I tell them it's because my husband is attending graduate school here. Sometimes I tell them it's because we're both freelance and can work from anywhere, and we picked here. Sometimes I tell them that for the last couple years we lived in Chicago I was clinging to a life that had stopped working in at least a dozen ways, even though I was unwilling to admit it to myself. Sometimes I say my whole world as I knew it fell apart, and right when we needed it, New York opened its arms to us in the most extraordinary way, that this city saved our lives. Sometimes I say I moved for love.

And every one of those answers is true.

For many months we lived in a swirl of confusion and shock, and every time we thought we'd reached the bottom, every time we thought the dust was clearing, something new exploded and it was like starting all over again—the disbelief, the anger, the sadness, the silence, the slow rise to finding a new normal . . . again.

It became clear that the church I loved—and that we were already in the process of leaving—could not be our church, and also our hometown couldn't continue to be our hometown. Staying felt cruel and unusual, like circling a cavern over and over, peering over the edge, looking at the empty space where your life used to be.

We knew we had to move, but we didn't know exactly where or when. We were living in the twilight zone. There's so much you don't know in the middle of it that becomes so very clear afterward, but then it was just a frozen horror, just getting through the days.

We had a trip to New York City that had been on the calendar for ages—the second summer trip of its kind, a little tradition beginning to emerge. We'd fly out on a Friday night, Sunday morning I'd preach and Aaron would lead worship at a church we both really liked, and then we'd stay for the rest of the week, celebrating the Fourth of July.

Sunday morning, I preached about darkness, because it was the only thing that felt honest. After church we had brunch at Soho House with a friend, and other friends from church invited us to their new apartment at a seminary in Chelsea. They told us to drop off our kids and go out for an early date. It was incredibly hot, and as we walked from Chelsea to the West Village, everyone we passed on the street was sweaty and wound up, the energy high on this Sunday afternoon, a holiday weekend, World Cup fans spilling out from every bar.

We ate at Buvette, one of my all-time favorite spots. I saw the chef, Jody Williams, downstairs and nervously told her how much I loved this special place she had created.

When we got back to the seminary, our friend David invited us to come over to his neighbors' house for a drink. When we sat down, Michael introduced himself to us as the academic dean and asked us what course of study we might be interested in here at the seminary. Aaron and I looked at each other and then at David, who burst out laughing and raised his glass. This was not a random neighbor, not a random introduction. David had been telling us he thought we should move to New York, to the seminary specifically, and in an extremely peak-David move, he orchestrated this moment toward that end without telling us anything.

We talked about faith and education, where we've come from. We talked about what we've left behind, what animates our dreams, what populates our vision for the future of the church and for our own lives. We went up to the rooftop and looked out over the city. Aaron and I kept stealing glances at each other—*Is this crazy, or is this a really significant conversation? Are you feeling this? Is this nuts?*

We didn't have a chance to debrief, because while we were talking with the dean, another friend texted and invited me to meet her later in the evening with friends. Her friend would be happy to get us into this new spot for some rosé and catching up.

What I expected: friends, rosé, catching up. What I did not expect: belly dancers, a tap-dancing Axl Rose impersonator, glow necklaces. The next morning, when Aaron went into the bathroom in the apartment where we were staying, he came out with a handful of glow necklaces that I'd taken off in there in the wee hours of the morning. "I have a lot of questions," he said. "I do too. I definitely do too," I said.

Now I know that that was a very New York day in a thousand little ways—that phenomenon of one adventure leading to another, one conversation or introduction connecting to another, like beads on a string. It's very New York to find yourself in five different neighborhoods in the course of a day and to walk about ten miles. Also, things got a little weird, and I stayed out later than I had in months and came home wearing a dozen glow necklaces for no good reason, and there's nothing more New York than that.

Weeks later, back at home, Aaron and I confessed to each other that we couldn't stop thinking about this seminary, those conversations, those dreams and ideas. The cocktail the dean made for us that night was called a Corpse Reviver. To call ourselves corpses would be going a step too far, but we were definitely, definitely in need of a little reviving.

seven

Kicking

A couple months before Henry's second birthday, we spent the afternoon on a boat in Saugatuck, Michigan, with several boats all rafted together, close enough to Coral Gables to hear the band playing on the upstairs deck.

Aaron was out of town, so I was extra conscious of being the solo parent, and we were with family and friends who either didn't yet have kids or had kids who were grown, so Henry was the only little one on all the boats. He wanted to go swimming, and I have to be honest that I wasn't dying to jump off the swim platform and paddle around with all these cool childless people watching me, but this is parenting, right?

So I jumped in and put out my arms for Henry to jump into them. He was a great little swimmer, and of course he was wearing an extremely aggressive Coast Guard–approved, extra-straps-and-handles life jacket—one of the side benefits of growing up in a sailing community. No one messes around with water safety. I held my arms out, and he jumped into them, and the weight of his little body pushed me below the surface of the water. I had a good grip on him and held my arms straight up, as high as I could. I kicked like crazy and held my breath. I started to panic but kept kicking, thinking that at a certain point I'd have enough power to get both our heads above water. I prayed he wouldn't freak out or wrestle out of my arms while his head was underwater. I prayed he would blow bubbles the way we practiced in shallow water. I kicked and kicked and pushed my arms higher and higher. I kept waiting for my head to break the surface, but it wasn't happening, and I was getting scared.

And then someone grabbed me around the waist and yanked me up, my head finally coming up from under the water. I gasped and sputtered. It was our friend Alex—Alex the Lion, we called him, like the movie *Madagascar*, because he was funny and exuberant and full of life and mischief. Henry loved him and was happy to curl into Alex's arms.

"What were you doing, Shauna? What on earth?"

"I know," I said. "I know it was dangerous. I know he was under for too long, and he was probably so scared."

"No," Alex said. "No. That's not what happened at all." He started to laugh. "Henry's feet weren't even in the water. *You* were under the water, but he wasn't even wet. He was just confused about why you wouldn't let him down into the water, and we were confused about why you were holding him up like Simba, and then we started to worry that you were going to drown yourself. We were yelling like crazy, but you couldn't hear us. That's when I jumped in."

Henry paddled around happily, and my brother and our friends jumped in and kept him entertained while I recovered my sanity, exhausted from what I thought was a near-death experience for both of us.

File under "Making it harder than it needed to be," which could be the title of everything I ever write, or everything I ever live. I can still feel the terror, the kicking, my arms burning, my legs working frantically beneath the surface until Alex came to gently rescue me and bring a halt to all my futile, ridiculous efforts. That feels like the story of my life over and over—expending insane amounts of energy, frantic and fearful, while all around me people are yelling, "I think it's going to be fine, pumpkin. I think you can stop kicking."

eight

Hello to Here

Last week my friend Julie came over for dinner and of course we talked books—my favorite topic besides food. She recommended Pádraig Ó Tuama's beautiful book *In the Shelter* and specifically mentioned one phrase that has captured me so deeply: "hello to here"—or I'm fully present to this here and this now, not the past or the future, not fantasies or regrets, but *here*.

A wise friend of mine says that true spiritual maturity is nothing more—and nothing less—than consenting to reality. *Hello to here*—not what you wanted or longed for or lost, not what you hope for or imagine. Reality. This here. This now.

These are the things I've always been writing about, the themes I've always been circling in one way or another. How does faith express itself in our blood-and-guts, sidewalks-and-streets daily lives? What does it mean to notice and bear witness to the ordinary moments of our lives—not the lofty ideas or peak experiences, but making sandwiches and making meaning and making a life, stitched together over time by all those moments of *here*?

What does it mean to be a noticer when what there is to notice is awful and you'd rather look away? What if your beautiful/ordinary everyday life isn't beautiful and hasn't been for a long time? For a long time, "hello to here" was an easy thing to say, like throwing a party for all the lovely parts of my life: hello, hello, hello. But all of a sudden, it was hard to say hello. It was hard to look the reality of my life full in the face. Here was not a place I wanted to be, and certainly not a place I wanted to greet enthusiastically.

Back, though, to spiritual maturity. Back to trying to roll my shoulders down. Back to unfeelable feelings and unthinkable thoughts. So many of us, especially Christians, especially women, have near-endless lists of things we're not allowed to think and feel, things we're never supposed to admit. Hunger and anger are at the top of that list. Jealousy. Rage. Despair. We've been told so often that other people have it so much worse, that we really have nothing to complain about, that we have to push through the pain. All those refrains for so long, and it's no wonder I can't feel anything except neck pain. I've been training all my life to pretend I'm fine and have let my body suffer for it.

Slowly, I became brave enough, little by little: hello to here. Hello to rage with sharp teeth. Hello to fear that felt bottomless. Hello to despair. Hello to heartbreak so visceral I felt it bodily, in my chest. I learned to breathe through it like labor pains, to stay with it and draw deep into my lungs, fearless and present to it, like a contraction. I learned to walk through it, my steps creating a drumbeat I could trust as the pain and sorrow and anger coursed through me, releasing block by block, footfall by footfall, drumbeat by drumbeat. To my surprise, instead of feeling overtaken, I felt cleansed, like the moment after a thunderstorm sweeps through and everything is suddenly impossibly quiet and clear.

I read and wrote and walked and listened and put my hand

on my heart, feeling the warmth of my palm stabilize me over time. Little by little, I became free and I became tender; I was newly sensitized to the pain so many people have been living with and bearing witness to for so long, and also to the pain I'd been carrying for a long time, within my own heart and body. Hello to here.

nine

Living Lightly

Moving to New York taught us that you don't need nearly as much space or as much stuff as you think. We moved from a house we'd been living in for ten years, in a town we'd been living in for the better part of our lives.

We sold and donated what seemed like acres of stuff. The house we had been living in wasn't a big house by Midwest standards, but it did have a basement and a garage, and as we started getting ready to move, we were absolutely flattened by how much *stuff* we had accumulated over the years.

We moved to New York to an 825-square-foot apartment, and everything we brought there fit into a 16-foot box truck. One set of silverware, one set of bowls. Twelve cloth napkins and, frankly, not nearly enough clothes. My friend Rachel, a makeup artist, was stopping over for something else one day before we moved, and I had all my makeup dumped on the dining room table. "Keep or toss, Rach?" I asked. And she deftly separated it all into two piles and told me I needed a new mascara.

Thank God for decisive friends, because at a certain point, I was just staring at things, squinting at them and trying to remember what the apartment actually looked like—we'd been in it for about half an hour two months before we moved in.

There's a lightness to how we live now that I appreciate. Nothing in our apartment got there by accident or neglect or just vague accumulation. We brought it a long way, very much on purpose, or we bought it once we arrived, realizing a specific need.

And the same is true for people. Another thing we're learning in this season is that you don't need nearly as many people as you might think. Not long after we moved, a family we love from Chicago came to visit, and we met them for rice pudding at Rice to Riches, and while we wandered Nolita afterward, my friend asked so delicately, "Do you have, um, enough friends here?" We laughed at the awkwardness of the question, and I thought about it for a minute.

"You know what?" I finally answered. "We do. There's a solid handful of people here who have been really good friends to us. And it's all we need—more than we need."

So much of the life I've lived up to this point was about holding things together, preserving them, never letting something fall or fall apart. It was like I was building a fortress, thick walls and foundations that went practically to the center of the earth itself. I was gathering people and years and traditions, wrapping people into it, weaving families and stories and moments and dinners together, trying to make something heavy and durable, something that would keep me safe.

And moving to New York taught me a million things about living more lightly—that you can love someone and learn from them and be deeply grateful for them for a season, and then bless their future. I saw glimpses of this before I left and noticed them because they were so counter to how I had lived.

We got to know a new family the year before we left because one of their daughters became good friends with one of our sons. They were new in town, from California, and we went to each other's houses for dinner a few times. I always talked about visiting each other or their kids coming to stay with us, and she always responded kindly but also in a way that told me, *Yeah, we're never doing that.* Not that they didn't like us. I think they did. But I saw every relationship, connection, family as something to be incorporated into this fortress—now you belong and you're in forever and please feel free to send your teenage daughter to stay with us in New York. What I should have said: *Thank you for dinner. I enjoyed being with you.* That's all.

There's a lovely foreign distance to city life. I like seeing our neighbors as we pass on the stairs, but then it's okay that they have dinner in one apartment and we have dinner in another. People like preserving a little space and privacy, because there's so little of it, relatively speaking. Mac's teachers were so fun and smart, and also anytime I asked them anything about their lives outside of school, they looked at me like I was a creeper. In my hometown, I knew the teachers and their kids and their neighbors. The guy who did my hair also did all my friends' hair.

We used to live in such a long-term way. My in-laws recently sold the house that Aaron's grandpa had built, that my father-in-law grew up in, that my in-laws had lived in for the last several years. Aaron and his siblings and cousins grew up spending holidays there, swimming in the pond. We'd celebrated birthdays and wedding showers and baby showers there. And then one day, we all went over there to clean out the attic and say our goodbyes. Seventy-five years of family history—five generations of memories and moments.

Six months later, we moved to a city where even the most committed city dwellers rent instead of own. I moved from a house we'd been in for nearly ten years that was on the same street I grew up on and the same street my brother lived on. From our living room window, I could see the roofline of the chapel of our church—layers upon layers, decades upon decades. And now we live in a city where people regularly move every year, and there's a lot to love about that.

When I was catching up with an old friend, telling him about our upcoming move, he said, "People like you never move away. I can't even picture it. You *were* your Chicago and your church and parties and dinners, and I can't even picture you living somewhere like New York City."

All I could say was, "I know, *I know*." We lived a really distinct, really special, very particular way for many years. And now we live an entirely different way, and I also love it. There are a lot of very good, very lovely ways to live, not right or wrong, just entirely different.

It's about having less stuff, and buying less stuff, and making a new relationship to stuff in general, but it's also about forgiveness—about how much anger and resentment you want to carry.

There have been stretches in the last couple years when I needed a wheelbarrow or even a semitruck to carry around all the anger and resentment I held on to. It was one of the core activities of my days, just keeping that anger and resentment alive and sparking, tending it like a fire. I'd think about it, talk about it, have imaginary conversations with the people involved, fantasize about spilling it all out onto the internet with glee. I knew I never would, but it was fun to imagine. But at a certain point, all that anger was like a pile of garbage in the middle of the floor of our apartment.

If we lived in a big house, maybe I could shove it all into a spare bedroom or a corner of the basement. But we need every square inch, and I can't afford all this garbage in here. And that's how I started to feel on the inside of myself, in my heart, like there just wasn't enough room for hope and gratitude, for life, really, because of all this garbage.

I know it might seem antithetical to move to the city that never sleeps in search of a smaller, quieter life. But that's what we've done. Less stuff, fewer relationships, and therefore fewer invitations and expectations. Less room to amass things, fewer places to hide. Just the four of us in a really small apartment, with as much as we can carry up and down three flights of stairs. We're learning what we don't need—a basement, a garage, cars. What we do need—a little shared green space, natural light, museum memberships. A couple good friends.

I'm not saying I'm thankful for all the things that broke apart in life as we knew it before, but I like our actual lives better—the day-to-day parts. They're lighter and more fun and more interesting. I know some things now, and I'm a lot less afraid of what might happen. I can make it through a lot. I know because I have.

I thought I needed a great army of friends, eleven sets of dishes, six pairs of boots, and two thousand books. I thought I needed an institution, a board of directors, a cozy blanket of like-minded, supportive people spread all over the country who would have my back in a heartbeat. Turns out you need three sweaters, rent money, and five really good people. You need eggs and coffee. A Kindle account, a metro card, and one good umbrella.

ten

Gravity of Love

On our first Sunday in New York, we sang a song at church called "Gravity of Love," and as we sang, I felt my eyes pool with tears—something about that beautiful song slid into that cavernous broken place inside me. For so many months I'd felt like I was in free fall, waiting to hit the bottom of everything, and in that moment, I realized there was a gravity even deeper than what I'd lost: the gravity of love. In that moment, a deep sense of God's love spilled into the cavern of my broken heart.

When I turned forty, the world as I understood it seemed strong. Stable. Impenetrable. Safe. I felt I was standing on solid ground, built over years and decades, a firm foundation of relationships and shared understandings, institutions I believed in and friendships and family relationships that kept me safe.

I wrapped all that around my shoulders like a blanket. I had no earthly idea that the blanket would unravel so thoroughly and so painfully.

It did not feel exhilarating or at all like freedom. It felt like I would die, like I'd been cut off from oxygen and had seconds, not minutes.

In those first months, I regularly found myself pressing a hand to my chest, hard, like I was trying to hold my heart, slow it or reassure it or something. I learned later that that's a technique used in body work and trauma recovery, and it doesn't surprise me at all that my body taught it to me without words.

Then that first Sunday, as we sang I cried, but it wasn't sadness; it was something like relief. Yes, yes, I knew that something or someone held me still. And yes, I knew it was love. And I felt held, for the first time in a long time. I put my hand on my chest, like I'd begun doing all those months ago, and I listened to the voices around me, and I cried with relief and gratitude.

There is gravity after all. There is a force that holds me. There is a central grounding of power, and that power is good. It is love. It is God.

It felt like I landed for the first time in a long time.

part two

Unbelonging

eleven

Buzz the Beach

One night in the deep freeze of winter, when it gets dark right around noon and stays that way for eight months, Henry and Mac and I were settling in to read in bed. As a desperate attempt to bring some brightness into the darkness of the season—the dark being both literal and metaphorical—I had wound copper-threaded twinkly lights through the black wrought iron headboard in our bedroom, and the light was soft and cozy.

As we snuggled up and opened our books, I asked them, "What do I always say?" The answer I was looking for was, "This is my favorite time of the day, pals!" I said it every time we snuggled up to read, and I meant it every time.

Mac, though, belted out an entirely different answer: *"Buzz the beach!"*

He was right. "Buzz the beach" is what I say all summer long when we're staying near the water, and it means going a couple minutes out of the way to see the water and the sky and the striped umbrellas and the sandy, happy beachgoers. I always want to buzz the beach—as a way of living, as a value, as a statement of faith.

I believe in seeking out beauty absolutely every chance we get, as an act of prayer, as an act of worship, as an act of resistance. I believe in going out of our way if it means getting to see the water or the mountains or the sky streaked with colors. I believe in attending the sunset the way some people buy fancy theater tickets.

The people I admire most are people who take celebration and memory making seriously. At my best, that's who I am: a moment maker, a noticer, a person who celebrates the tiny goodnesses of our lives.

I officiated a wedding for good friends, and later, after the wedding was over, after Aaron and I were back at the hotel and I'd taken off my heels and tights and was eating almond cake in bed, I finally had a chance to read the program and found, to my great delight, that I was listed as "Officiant with a side of sparkle"—that is officially my favorite title of all time.

It's easy, of course, to buzz the beach and find the sparkle on good days—days when the sun is shining and your heart is light. When it gets really dark, though, that's when you start to understand that it's a discipline, and you need it in the dark so much more desperately than you need it in the light. Joy and celebration are practices for the long haul.

Whenever possible, walk out of your way for a few minutes and take a few deep breaths somewhere beautiful—whether that's a forest clearing or a French bakery or a path through a prairie or a cobblestone street. Take the long way sometimes, reveling in the discovery of beauty, noticing everything you can—what it smells like and the slant of the light and how the sounds remind you of recess or Rome or Grand Rapids.

In the recovery movement, you often hear the phrase "it works if you work it." I feel the same way about faith, about inspiration, about joy. It's a gift, and also it's a giving, a receiving and extending, a partnership of effort from both parties.

I buzz the beach because I take my role in a joy-filled life very seriously. I want to be a person of great joy, and I'm not waiting around for someone else to deliver it to me. I participate in my own healing, in my own inspiration, in my own practice of hope.

I drive out of my way to see the beauty and chaos of the crowded beach, the umbrellas and babies and teens splashing each other and yelping, because the beach puts me in the path of joy, and I believe that work to be part of my responsibility to myself, to my community, and to the God who made it all and sustains it all. It's a way of saying thank you. It's a way of reflecting my love and gratitude toward the Creator, and a way of acting out my belief that "wasting" time is sometimes a deeply meaningful spiritual practice.

I buzz the beach because the time we spend making memories is never wasted, because nature reminds us that we're part of a bigger whole, and that beauty matters and so does play. I buzz the beach because I want to live out my belief that there are more important things to do in a given day than to complete our to-do lists. I buzz the beach because even on the worst days, even on the darkest days, the waves still come in and then recede, the wind still blows, the sun—that drama queen—still puts on a performance every night.

twelve

The Best Mistake

In the season before we moved, one of my greatest concerns was for our boys. A good friend—and recent acquirer of a puppy—told me a puppy would bring our boys happiness and love every day, that they would thrive with something to take care of, play with, something to bring them joy.

I would have brought home a dinosaur if I thought it would bring them some joy, and so when they started talking about a puppy, I was listening. We found a breeder we loved—many people encouraged us toward a rescue, and we loved the idea of that, of course, but also Mac and I have pretty serious allergies, as do lots of extended family members, so we felt we couldn't necessarily risk the unknowns of a rescue. We emailed and researched and made plans.

We knew we were probably moving, and we thought a dog would be a good point of consistency for the boys—in a season of so much change, this little guy would be with us throughout the ups and downs. We thought we'd get the puppy early in the summer. We thought maybe we'd move after the New Year, giving us six or eight months of puppy life before a move.

And then, just like life, all our hypotheses about how the moving process and timeline would go went out the window several times over. When the puppy we had planned on was born, our breeder reached out to say she thought we might be allergic to him, and to be on the safe side, we should wait for the next litter. Then our house sold much more quickly than we had planned, and also the apartment we were moving to in New York was available earlier than we had planned, and we realized we'd be paying rent on it and also paying to rent back our own house if we stayed with the current after-the-New-Year plan.

All that to say, what we envisioned being six or eight months of pre-move puppy life became one extremely chaotic month, and in addition to having never lived in a city and having never lived in an apartment, we arrived in Manhattan to an apartment we'd seen once, with a box truck of furniture . . . and a twelve-week-old puppy. In November.

Sgt. Pepper is an adorable red Australian Labradoodle, medium-sized, but especially when he was a puppy, he looked just like a teddy bear. He is darling and smart and sweet, and if you ever want to meet people in a new city, by all means, get a puppy. Grown men and women would lie down on the sidewalk on Twentieth Street to let Pep crawl all over them and lick their faces. We became puppy pals with every dog in Chelsea, it seemed—and there were a lot. We met Sprout and his parents and Monster and his parents, and we always stopped to say hello to George and his mom—they were regulars at the High Line Hotel lobby bar and coffee shop, the very stylish spot at the end of our block, and we became regulars too, because the main bartender, Michael, fell in love with Sgt. Pepper and when it wasn't busy, he'd come out from behind the bar and play with Pepper for ages. Anyone who was willing to help wear out our puppy was a forever friend in my book, and still when I think about our first New York weeks, I think about coming in from the cold to that cozy bar and Michael's delight at seeing Sgt. Pepper.

Here's what we didn't know: in New York, pet-friendly means something different than it does other places. For example, our apartment was "pet-friendly," so we imagined long, lazy afternoons in the courtyard, playing fetch with Pep, or him snuggling up at our feet on the lawn while we read in the Adirondack chairs. We were quickly disabused of this notion, because in New York "grass is for people." It makes sense now, after some time here, and I do understand that no one wants to stretch out on a patch of rare green space only to find it freshly peed upon, but this was a major mind-bender for us early on.

So it was perfectly fine for the puppy to be in our apartment. But he had to be on a leash at all times anywhere on the campus, and he could never go on the grass. Ever. And also, here in New York, dogs go potty by hanging their back ends off the curb and going in the street, between parked cars. The first hundred times we took Pep out to the curb, he looked up at us like, *I know I'm a baby, but you think I don't know you're asking me to pee in the street? What is this place? Who are you people?* We didn't know either, bud. We didn't know either.

There were dog parks, but they were just gated areas with various concrete elevations, sort of like a cross between a prison yard and an abandoned skatepark. And there were days and times when dogs were welcome in various parks for off-leash time, but the logistics of getting a dog to said park for the allotted window was a challenge well beyond our capacity at that point.

We timed all of our excursions around letting Pepper out, but we barely knew the city and definitely didn't understand the subway system, so about half the time, Aaron or I would run ahead or leave dinner early or sprint home to make sure the poor pup got out in time to go potty—it was like that one season of *Lost* where they have to keep entering the numbers, even though they don't really know what would happen if they didn't. It was like living with a tiny, furry, ticking time bomb.

The boys loved Pep, and so did Aaron and I . . . but also it seemed that Pepper had formed an early attachment to me that I can only describe as a soul mate–level connection. He followed me everywhere I went; he watched me all the time; he gazed longingly at me wherever I was in the apartment or lay behind a closed door and whined for me if I had the audacity to, say, go to the bathroom without him. Our tiny kitchen has a pantry that is definitely not a walk-in, but I definitely started walking into it and closing the door behind me, just for a little space from the lovable stalker.

I know what you're thinking: *Train that dog. Take that dog to obedience school.* Yes. Yes, I know. We did take him to a puppy class—in the middle of the icy, sleeting winter, a full mile from our apartment. The other dogs in the class were all two to five pounds, and their owners acted like we had brought a Clydesdale to stomp their babies. It did not go well.

At one point, Pep had a diarrhea/vomiting combo that meant we were running him down three flights of stairs, across the courtyard, down more stairs, across the sidewalk, and onto the curb, just in time for him to poop brown water for a while— and then reversing the process back up to the apartment, where, upon arrival, he'd vomit.

I took him to the vet, where they ran a battery of tests that cost more than two thousand dollars. The tests confirmed that he had not, in fact, eaten a sock, but they recommended a few days of organic boiled chicken and white rice. You cannot imagine how delighted I was to add "make organic boiled chicken and white rice three times a day for a DOG" to my current to-do list, which also contained items like "get health insurance" and "buy a kitchen table."

After three months—the coldest on record for New York City for the last number of years—my mom called and said, "I have to tell you something. I'm watching you, and I'm watching this situation, and something needs to change. There's a lot I can't solve here, but I can make one thing easier: I'll take the dog for a while."

And I sobbed. I never would have asked her. I hadn't even thought of it. Sgt. Pepper was just one more part of our crazy new life in New York, and I hadn't even had a moment to step back and ask myself if there were ways to make our life here a little easier or a little more workable. But she had, and she had a plan.

She reminded me on the phone that there was a generational precedent for this, a history repeating itself. When my brother and I were little and my dad was traveling a lot, my brother was shy and not a great sleeper, and my grandma, my mother's mother, told my mom, "You need to get that boy a dog." My mom did, and Buster proved to be a great companion for Todd . . . but also kind of a handful. He chewed through every pair of shoes in the house—once he even chewed a hole through a dinner guest's shoe while he was wearing it, without him noticing what was happening. My mom took Buster to obedience school, but he was asked to leave midterm, because not only was he not making the required progress, but he was disrupting the progress of the other dogs.

My grandma said, "Okay, bring him over to Michigan for a while. He can live with us for a little bit, and we can get him on a good schedule because we're retired and we can give obedience school another try here, and when he's a little older, he can come home."

That's what they did, and it made all the difference, and so my mom said she had her mom's voice in her ears as she called me. And that's how Sgt. Pepper went to stay with my parents for a while. A month, I thought, or at the very outside, until we went to visit them in the summer.

My parents called with frequent updates, and it seemed like things were going fine, but I was concerned that they weren't telling me how hard it was or that they were sort of "grinning and bearing it" for my sake. My brother called at a certain point, and I asked him to give it to me straight. Is this too hard for them? Am I taking too much? Is it time for him to come back?

Todd said, "Shauna, I'm going to tell you something. I don't think that dog's ever coming back to New York." I didn't understand.

"What?" I asked. "Is something wrong? Is he sick? Are they getting rid of him?"

"No," he said. "I think they've fallen in love with him. I think our parents just got a dog."

As the months went on, it became clear that this little dog was absolutely living his best life, with two retired people, lots of land, and unlimited snuggles and treats. They live in an extremely dog-friendly town, and walking to the store or a restaurant with him is like being in the presence of a celebrity. He is the happiest, smartest, sweetest little guy, and he has the undivided attention and adoration of half the town.

When we were visiting that first summer, I overheard a conversation between Mac and my mom. My mom is a fundamentally gentle and generous person who rarely speaks forcefully, especially with my kids. Which is why I was surprised to hear this exchange. Mac said, "You know, Sgt. Pepper is my dog, but it's pretty cool that he gets to live with you."

My mom looked Mac in the eye and said, "Mac, Sgt. Pepper is *my* dog."

And that was that. We get to visit and get our fill of snuggles, and we get to watch with amusement as my parents have become truly obsessive dog parents, and Sgt. Pepper is living a life of splendor and joy.

I've made so many mistakes over the past few years—some big and some small, some rather inconsequential and some quite grave. But here's what I do know: had we suggested to our parents that a puppy might be a good addition to their life in this season, they would have looked at us like we were insane. But sometimes our biggest mistakes turn into weird, unexpected gifts, and Sgt. Pepper is one. I know it doesn't always happen like that, and I've made plenty of mistakes that have to get made right in complicated, painful, laborious ways.

That's most of the time. But every once in a while, because God is just that good and life is just that good, some of our mistakes get turned upside down into delight and joy and puppy love, and in a season of so much loss and darkness, I'll take it.

thirteen

Waiting for Daylight

I believe in the light, in the dawn, in the dancing that comes after sorrow, but I am living right now in the dark. Some of the most treasured things in my life turned to dust in my hands, and in my best moments I know that new life will come, that the dawn will indeed break, but right now, my heart and spirit have been carrying a heavy weight, a dark weight, for many months. And I know I'm not the only one.

I know we have lost loved ones, and we have walked through illness and suffering together. I know that treasured relationships have ended, jobs we've loved are no more. I know that many of us feel exhausted and outraged at the state of our nation. We've endured the death of dreams, the loss of optimism. We've watched our children and our parents struggle. We've walked alongside people we love as they've battled addiction and struggled to find solid ground and enduring mental health. We've prayed for the dawn, ached for light, for a break, for healing of many kinds. We've struggled to remain hopeful, but many of us find ourselves, in different ways, living in profound darkness.

Many years ago, a pastor friend of mine told me that the central narrative of Christianity is death and new life, over and over, death and new life. Some traditions call this narrative the

Paschal Mystery. But when this pastor, many years ago, talked with me about it, I argued with him. "I don't think so," I said.

"Great, then," he said, "tell me what you think it is."

"Life," I said. "More life, then more life, then you grow, then you learn, then more life."

"Sure, sure," he said. "What about, you know, the cross? Was that a pain-free learning experience?"

"Okay," I said, "you got me."

And over the years since that conversation, I've come back to his words again and again. And I see it everywhere. Death makes way for life. The winter yields to the spring. The night brings the dawn. This is reality. I'm terrible at accepting it, but I'm trying.

Pain is pain and there's no use comparing—in particular, there's no use saying what you've been through isn't bad enough. There's no rating system, no Olympics of suffering. Dark is dark, period, but one way we distract ourselves from our own pain is by getting really concerned with everyone else's pain. You become like a traffic cop for other people's journeys—*Oh, you think that's bad? Oh, please, it's barely dark where you are. Cry me a river.* This is not helpful. Not for you, not for them.

And if you're in the midst of a painful season, don't feel guilty for catching yourself feeling happy every once in a while. That's not wrong. That's not betraying the loss. Let yourself be sad and then angry and then laugh really hard. Let yourself be tired and then anxious and then let yourself be surprised by a moment of beauty, of joy. This is how it is in the dark— confusing and circuitous and absolutely all the things some- times, even in the same day.

I'm also learning that it never helps to pretend everything's okay. Putting on a brave face doesn't help anyone. Just this week, I forced myself to tell the truth to a small circle of friends I trust like sisters. I told them all of it, all the way. That was difficult—and a little embarrassing.

I wanted to give them a show-offy progress report of how swimmingly I was handling everything. I wanted to be the superstar of the darkness—*I love it here. This is great. I'm nailing this.* But I'm not. I need help. And I got the help and support I needed because I reached out in a super-messy way.

Bring all the wreckage to people you trust. I know it's awful to be seen in all your suffering. I have hidden from my friends in my own house when they have stopped over to check on me, only to realize that, because I'd forgotten the front door was open, they could see me hiding. Like a toddler who covers her eyes and says, "You can't see me." I'm so thankful that people who love me came into my house and saw me, right in the suffering. Because that's how we get through.

Allow yourself to be helped and supported by friends and family, invitations to walk together or share a meal, intercessory and healing prayer. And let's also not forget counseling and therapy and medication and spiritual direction and retreat and a million other things we might receive to keep us company along the way. Let's leave behind any remaining stigma or unhelpful stereotype about counseling or therapy—what a gift God has given us in counselors and therapists, our guides through the darkness, our wise companions as we wait for the dawn.

Let's build meaningful, supportive, honest scaffolding around one another as we struggle against life's challenges, as we wait for the dawn together. Let's create an authentic and open conversation about mental health, about depression, addiction, despair, loneliness, doubt, and loss of faith. Let's help each other through the dark. Offer to listen, to walk, to share a meal. And if someone offers that to you, as difficult as it is, accept it. Because no one gets through the night alone.

When you don't know how to help yourself, help someone else. Loss or pain or suffering can turn you inward. It's all-consuming sometimes. But it's so helpful sometimes to show up, even in small ways, for someone else. Serve someone. Help someone. Give something to someone, and the doing so will remind you that the world is still turning beyond your loss. It is, even when it seems like it can't be.

Look for the good, even in the dark—especially in the dark. Once you train your eyes for tiny glimpses of goodness, you'll get better at seeing them, and you'll see more and more and more. And they'll keep you company and keep your heart tender as you long for daylight.

I am not at all suggesting that you should say, *I'm so glad this happened, because* . . . I'm talking about being the kind of person who asks, even as you are grieving the death of many beloved things, even in the night, *Who has cared for me well? Who has been kind? Where have I felt able to rest or be seen? In the middle of the darkness, where have I seen redemption or bravery or tiny bits of hope?*

The practice of gratitude keeps our hearts tender through the night instead of allowing bitterness and cynicism to take over. Choosing to see the good right in the middle of the darkness and loss is a discipline, and I'm finding it to be a life-changing one.

Today my friend Julia left a loaf of still-warm sourdough in a bag hanging on our doorknob and I didn't actually cry but I very, very almost did, because when everything feels like a wreck, small kindnesses can change everything. A loaf of bread, a text, a moment of connection. A walk together, a phone call, a pint of berries left on a porch, a care package shipped to a faraway friend.

My friend's kindness nourished me when I didn't even realize how starved I was, and you'd better believe we're going to eat this whole loaf today, with truly egregious amounts of salted butter.

fourteen

Healing in the Trying

One of my best friend's brothers was ordained as a priest in the Roman Catholic Church recently, and she came over a few weeks later to show me all the pictures of the ceremony. One of the things she mentioned to me is now that Robert is a priest, there is an expectation that he will say a Mass every day. Every single day.

When I first heard this, I understood it as sort of a logistics thing: he's placed in a parish, and if that parish offers daily Mass and he's the only priest, he's doing daily Mass. But that's not it at all, she explained to me. She said it's not about the parish. It's not about the congregants needing to receive a Mass. It's about the belief that it's best for the priest to practice his vocation every single day, to keep him connected to what God has called him into, and to deepen that connection every single day.

So for the rest of his life, Robert will find a church and say a Mass every day—when he's in Vietnam, or when he's in Central America, or when he's in his own parish in Louisville, Kentucky.

In my own life, I've found that when the darkness has been at its most engulfing, some of the most healing moments have come when I have embraced and acted out my own callings, even in small or fumbling ways. The twin callings on my life are storytelling and hospitality. In our family, sometimes we call them chatting and snacks. I gather people, create safe and restorative spaces for them, and tell the truth about who God is and what he does in our daily blood-and-guts, streets-and-sidewalks lives. Those are the things I'm made to do.

Writing and gathering people bring me back to life, even when I'm sure they won't, even when I desperately don't want to do either. I learn over and over again that an hour of writing or a last-minute gathering can revive me in ways nothing else can. They bring about my own healing and a renewed perspective, right when I need it most.

It's very easy when you're in the dark, when you're longing for daylight, to stop practicing those things because everything feels hard and who knows if those things even matter anymore and nothing feels right and so you stop.

I read a great novel earlier this year called *How to Walk Away* by Katherine Center, one of my favorite novelists. It was totally unrelated to anything I was experiencing—it was actually about a woman with a spinal cord injury—but something that her physical therapist said caught me. He said the healing is in the trying. *The healing is in the trying.*

I don't know when the dawn will break, for you or for me, but I know that the healing comes in the trying and that even in the dark we have to keep practicing our callings, whatever they are. We have to keep doing the things we were made to do, the daily acts of goodness and creativity and honesty and service—as much for what they bring about inside us as for the good they do in the world. Those two things work together, and they both matter.

Practice your vocation or calling, whatever you understand that to be, because the practice of it will keep you connected to your own deepest self and to the God who planted those gifts inside you. Because this is how life is. We get stuck in the dark, sometimes for a long time. We ache for morning. And sometimes it seems like it will never come.

But this is also how life is. Dawn always breaks. Morning always comes.

fifteen

Unbelonging

The last several years have been a near-constant process of unbelonging—untethering from the places and people and ideas that have held my identity for so long.

I'm a belonger, a joiner, a deeply loyal person who would prefer to live surrounded by a raft of old friends, family members, inside jokes, shared traditions. I'd like to be advised on all major decisions by a personal board of directors. I love Mafia movies. Growing up, I wanted to be Jewish or Italian or Catholic, to have a sense of that connection and identity.

To my great horror, the first part of my forties has been an unwinding of the threads that wrapped around my life, a throwing off of all the lines, a systematic and painful series of unbelongings. I didn't choose the unbelongings—by that I mean it wasn't strength or independence or boldness. It was more someone peeling my fingers, one by one, away from the life I'd been clutching with white knuckles, the life that didn't fit anymore, no matter how hard I was trying to hold on.

I know I'm not alone in this experience—in recent years a good friend left the political party that had been like a religion to her since childhood. So many friends have found their relationship to the church to be increasingly untenable because of the church's positions on sexuality, race, gender, and politics.

I have friends whose marriages have ended after decades, friends who no longer speak to family members because of political divides. We have friends moving to other countries because they no longer have faith in the future of this country.

What I know now is I am able to stand, even without the scaffolding of belonging I've depended so heavily on. It's a little like stepping down onto your foot after the cast has been removed, holding your breath for just a second as you test the newly repaired bones. The bones support you, and you can hardly believe it. Another step, then another.

Resilience is, simply put, getting back up. It's getting back up, not just after the first fall, but the ninth and tenth and seven hundredth. Resilience is feeling your exhaustion and choosing to move forward anyway. Resilience is watching your lovingly made plans fall to dust in your hands, grieving what's lost and making (yet another) plan. It's being willing to lay down your expectations for what you thought your life would be, what this year would be, what this holiday season would be, and being willing to imagine another way.

I had to learn a deeper level of resilience skills in the last few years, and this is what I know: It gets easier. It gets easier to get back up the more you do it. It gets easier to grieve what's gone and look honestly into the face of what remains the more often you have to do it. This is the way through.

Every single time throughout your life that you've hit the ground hard and fought to get back up will help you now. And every time you get back up in this season, it will build inside you the resilience you'll need for the next season, whatever that is. It's good news / bad news. I'm sorry we're having to learn so much about resilience right now—that's the bad news. The good news: nothing is wasted. Your discipline, your creativity, your stubborn hope—they're changing you, little by little. And the next season of great pain and challenge will be just a little easier because of these hard choices you're making now.

Earlier this year, I felt like I couldn't find the rhythm, like I was underwater. I was trying, but I was all over the place, false starts and faltering steps, self-doubt, self-sabotage. Wild-minded, sleepless. All I could do was keep putting one foot in front of the other, doing the good things that I know yield good living—including but not limited to walking, reading, therapy, writing, prayer, silence, connection, water, sleep. One foot in front of the other, slogging through.

And then finally yesterday at church, near the end of the gathering, I realized that the ground beneath my feet felt solid again, for the first time in too long. And it was a reminder to me that there are no quick fixes, no overnight successes, that everything good and worthwhile takes time, and generally way more time than we like to imagine. Good things take time.

I know what it's like to have your heart broken. And also, I know what it's like to forgive, little by little, over and over, a little more each day. I know what it's like to breathe fresh clean air again after a long stretch of choking on the fumes of anger.

And I know now that I can trust myself, that I can belong to myself, that belonging to something larger than myself is lovely but isn't for every season. It's a little lonelier out here, a little rockier. I'm learning to make myself a home in the wilderness, in the unbelonging itself.

sixteen

Learning to Let Go

When my cousin Melody and I were six years old, our dads decided to teach us to water-ski on Lake Michigan. Which, for the non-water-skiers among us, is not really where you want to begin that journey. Water-skiing is usually best on smaller lakes or inland lakes with flat water and minimal traffic—basically the exact opposite of Lake Michigan. But it was early in the morning and the lake was glassy and our dads were excited.

I was excited too, but Melody was categorically not interested until they spoke her love language: cash. Uncle Dan told Mel he'd give her five bucks if she could get up on those water skis. The sentence was barely out of his mouth before she was in the water.

After a few tries, she got up, she skied along for about thirty seconds, staring evenly at her dad in the back of the boat, and then she let go of the rope and sank slowly into the water.

We hooted and hollered and cheered as she swam back to the boat—"Way to go, Mel! You were great! But why did you let go? Want to go again?"

"Nope," she said. "Where's my money?" And as far as I know, she's never skied again.

I took a slightly opposite approach. When they explained it to me, they kept saying, "The rope is going to want to pull out of your hands, but don't let it! Don't let go! Whatever you do, don't let go."

And so on my first try, the rope indeed pulled me forward, past standing position, until I was flat on my stomach, face skimming along the water. My skis fell off, but I did not let go of the rope. My face was bouncing in and out of the water, but I did not let go of the rope. They yelled and waved their arms—"Let go! Honey, let go!" But I couldn't hear them because my ears were mostly under the water. And so they dragged me until they could get to a point where they could make a wide turn, and then when I swam up to the boat, waterlogged and coughing, they were confused. "What were you doing out there, Shauna?"

"You told me not to let go. So I didn't." And that's basically a snapshot of how I've lived for the intervening fortyish years: not letting go—also, occasionally being dragged.

Last summer, I heard the phrase "let go or be dragged," and I felt it in every fiber of my being. The phrase is a Zen proverb, and it put words to an experience I had over and over again in the last several years. There are some people who leave early, and others who have a tendency to overstay, and I am an over-stayer of the most extreme kind and have lived that way for most of my life. One of the most central learnings of midlife is learning how to let go.

And living in New York has given me a lot of practice, because people are always leaving. Our friends who are pastors say that's the worst part of pastoring in New York, and teachers and principals everywhere are well versed in first days and last days, every school year.

Barbara and I met for the first time in December, for the last time in June, and in those intervening hours and months she told me stories about her life and listened to stories about mine. She answered a thousand of my questions and held tender space for my tears and anger. I was just arriving in New York, and she was preparing to leave after more than forty years here.

She was a priest, a professor, a spiritual director, a great-grandmother. She was married to a celebrated English professor, and together they were moving to Boulder, Colorado, where her daughters now lived. Many years ago, she had a best friend who lived in the apartment we live in now. He died of AIDS, she told me, like so many young men in this neighborhood in the eighties. She told me that when they were seminary students together, stressed-out and overtired during finals, they had pillow fights.

I attended a retreat she led and read several of her books, but most of what I know about her is what she shared with me during spiritual direction on the eleventh floor of a stuffy building on Fifth Avenue, next to Marble Collegiate Church. The first time I met her there, it was raining and I had forgotten an umbrella but walked the fifteen blocks anyway. I turned up so thoroughly soaked I looked like I'd been swimming.

I was reeling from a big move and so much loss, trying to find my way in a new city, a new church, a new life in every way. She was leaving a city where she'd been known for decades, a legend in some ways, much admired and well loved. We talked a lot about transition, about seasons, about leaving things behind and letting things die, even though we had loved them so dearly.

I think of her when I walk down Fifth Avenue or stop in the big classroom on the east end of the seminary, and I think of her sometimes when I pray, because at the end of our time together we would pray together, an intimate and tender thing. She was a little prickly and incredibly wise, and she'd known a lot of pain in her life and also a lot of joy. We shared a city for less than a year, and every moment of it felt like a gift to me.

seventeen

Enchantment

Not long after we moved to New York, a new friend asked about my design style as it pertains to homes and spaces. I struggled with what to say, starting several sentences, making half statements, breaking off halfway through three times in a row, and then finally I said, "You know what? I'm not sure right now."

I knew what it had been, certainly. Before we moved, I could have told you with great clarity exactly what my design style was—mostly classic, a touch masculine, neutrals and blues, metallics. A bazillion books, lots of artwork and photographs, and strings of lights year-round, not just at Christmas. Navy, stripes, grays. Nautical details, French accents, lots of musical instruments. A home where creative people live, warm but not cluttery.

The home we lived in for ten years reflected that perfectly—gray walls and floors, navy cabinets. Lots of leather furniture and bookcases. And then we came here, and all of a sudden, this all-gray-and-navy girl started feeling pulled like a magnet to things that are red and bright green, vintage things, silly things, the brighter the better.

These days I can't get enough—color, pattern, play. Plaid and gingham and ikat and florals. I have a new obsession with block print, the brighter the better. The last pillow I bought is a near-neon traditional Mexican embroidery from the Frida Kahlo exhibit at the Brooklyn Museum. Something about the architecture, the history, the city itself awakened something colorful and playful inside me.

The exterior of our building is red brick with hunter-green trim, and I think that's part of what makes me want our space to feel like a cozy, creative college professor's office. I want gold-leaf frames and portraits of horses, vintage dishes and throws on the arms of every chair. Also, a whole lot of elaborate Lego creations and a rose-gold disco ball. These days, I don't care so much about a consistent design aesthetic. These days, I want to be enchanted.

It's okay to let yourself change, to let an environment change you, a city change you, a season change you. You are who you are, and also it's okay to love one thing and then another.

And that's the point—it's not about pillows; it's about the freedom and joy that come with letting yourself reimagine almost everything. When I look back now, I think about how extremely well defined my whole world was. This kind of car. This kind of food. This is how I dress. This is how our house looks. This kind of church. This kind of life, really.

But now it isn't. And I like that. I like the permission and freedom and creativity this reimagining brings into bloom in every area of life.

A new city, and with it new traditions and patterns. Henry's a diner guy—his ideal meal is a burger and a strawberry milk-shake at a diner that has been open for decades. His other favorite place to visit is a bookstore, the smaller and quirkier the better. I keep a running list of best diners and best book-stores around the city, and every few weeks, we cross one more diner and one more bookstore off the list. Last night, we went to

Joe Jr. on Third Avenue. Henry likes his burgers with ketchup only, so I end up with double the tomato/lettuce/pickle—lucky me. Also lucky me—I get to go to diners and bookstores with this smart, creative, funny, kind kid.

Before the pandemic, I heard my favorite child psychologist and parenting expert Wendy Mogel speak at Lincoln Center. She was wonderful and wise and I took pages of notes, and she said something that stayed with me, something I think about almost every day: "I've been seeing worried parents for decades now. Parents worry, and kids are mostly fine. Just do this one thing: Be enchanted by whatever's currently enchanting your child."

So we go to diners and bookstores. We watch bazillions of movies, because film is Henry's greatest passion. Mac and I make "Sunday Sauce" any day of the week if he gets it in his head that it's sauce-making day, because in his heart, he believes he's a little Italian (I mean, don't we all?).

This idea of enchantment is parenting gold, certainly, but it also has so much to bring to all our relationships. Aaron is a fifth-generation Cubs fan, and part of being his partner is loving what he loves. I mean, okay, there are some things he loves that I love for him but do not love myself ('90s grunge, golf, Shark Week), but I went all in on baseball.

We went to a couple games a year, initially, and watched some on TV. And then I started to really get into it. I started to learn the terminology and learn my way around Wrigley Field, and then in our trickiest season of marriage, that love for the Cubs and Wrigley Field became a safe zone for us, a reminder of all that connected us even while it seemed so many things were coming between us.

One night this summer, Aaron's sister Emily and I broke off

from the whole family conversation, and for about an hour, just the two of us huddled together on the couch in the living room while the rest of the family hung out in the family room. When we finally ended our conversation, someone asked, "Good girl talk?" "Yes," we said, "we did a pretty deep dive on the Cubs trade deadline." They cracked up because they thought we were kidding, but we spent every second of that hour talking about the implications of losing this player or that one, how trades in recent years had changed the team, how hard it is to watch favorite players leave. I got into this baseball thing for Aaron, but I'm pretty well enchanted by it myself these days.

I love that phenomenon, that we go through life falling in love with new things because of the people we love, because of the paths they lead us down. I've watched a hundred movies I never would have watched because Henry wanted me sitting next to him for those couple of hours, and there's nowhere else I'd rather be. I love the neighborhoods I've discovered with my walking buddy Jennifer, and the books that have become treasured favorites that my summer camp friend Laura recommended to me. I find that beautiful process of learning and discovery downright enchanting.

eighteen

Our First New York-iversary

For JRW

During a busy stretch of travel, I came down with what seemed like a bad cold and fever. It's definitely something I should have paid more attention to, but I didn't, for all sorts of reasons—I didn't have a doctor here yet, and I was traveling and figured it would go away. Also the general chaos and challenge levels of our life were pretty high.

But it got worse instead of better, and finally after ten nights of a very high fever, waking up alternately drenched or teeth-chatteringly cold, Aaron intervened and bundled me into an Uber to an urgent care we found online. It was a truly terrible place, but a smart and kind doctor talked me through my symptoms and the lab took copious blood work. I mentioned to the doctor that I had a long-scheduled appointment with a new ob-gyn the next day, but if I still felt so terrible, I'd cancel it. "Keep it," he encouraged me. "You need a doctor in the city, and the more info we can get about what's causing this high fever, the better."

I went to that appointment the next day, and the doctor was quite glamorous—sort of a Jackie Kennedy vibe with a soft Russian accent. She asked a new midwife to do an internal ultrasound. The midwife poked around for a while and then finally said, "I'm sorry, I've done a thousand of these, but they're always on pregnant women. I'm having trouble finding her ovaries." The doctor leaned closer and peered at the screen and said, "Oh yes. That's because they're so tiny and shrunken."

The doctor turned to me and asked how long I'd been in menopause. I was confused. "No," I said, "I'm just sick. I just have this fever."

She said, "We'll talk about this later. Your fever's too high. I think you're in danger of going into sepsis, and I want you to go straight from here to the ER at Lenox Hill."

What on earth? Menopause? Shrunken ovaries? Sepsis? ER? Also, there was still a midwife hunting for my tiny, shrunken ovaries via internal ultrasound.

I texted Aaron to meet me at the ER, and by the time the medical team did my intake, I was indeed in sepsis, and they wheeled me back and began all sorts of tests. After several hours, they were able to rule out most things and lower my fever a little, but not enough, so several hours later, they admitted me to a double room on one of the higher floors. Aaron needed to go to be with the kids, and I curled up into a ball in my room and waited to go to sleep.

I was in the bed closest to the door, which meant that anyone going to the patient by the window walked right past my bed. And the patient by the window was in serious pain and needed near-constant care. People were in and out all day and all night, and there was screaming and crying, and in the moments when her pain was stabilized, she asked me a whole lot of very personal questions through the curtain, but that seemed fair, I guess, because I was listening in on her very personal medical processes. It was awful.

I texted an out-of-town friend, and like friends do, she quickly assessed what was happening. "Are you doing that thing you do where you sort of shut down and isolate and pretend you're okay and you don't reach out for help even though you clearly need it?"

That's exactly what I was doing. We had a mutual friend in New York—but one she knew much better than I did. She made me promise to text Jennifer right away.

Jennifer came first thing the next morning with fruit and an egg sandwich and a stack of magazines. She sat on my bed with me, and this was a major jump for us. We were meet-at-a-restaurant friends. We were decidedly not snuggle-up-in-my-horrible-hospital-bed friends—at least we weren't until then.

The woman on the other side of the curtain started screaming again, and the procedures she needed were invasive and loud. Jennifer mouthed to me, "Has it been like this all night?" I nodded, and she said, "I'll be back in a minute."

I don't know who she talked to or what happened, but within an hour I was in a private room with a window.

Later that night, while changing my IV, one of the nurses mentioned that some intravenous medicines need to be administered more slowly than others because of how hard they are on the system. She explained that they have to take into account the kind of medicine, the amount needing to be given, and the size of the veins.

I listened to all this while looking at the ceiling and breathing heavily through my nose because veins are not my best thing, and a detailed discussion about the amount of harsh chemicals pumping through my actual veins is basically my nightmare situation.

"You've got to be careful," she said. "You don't want to blow out a vein, do you?" I almost threw up in my mouth, but instead I nodded. "Yep, that's what I always say: I don't want to blow out a vein."

Several hours later, in the middle of the night, I woke up because my arm was wet, liquid spilling and running down my arm onto the bed and sheets and floor. I thought, in my sleep-soaked brain, that it was condensation from my water glass, but it was, in fact, a combination of my own blood and the intravenous medicine flowing freely from my blown-out vein. Like one of my actual nightmares. By the time I went home a few days later, I was bruised from elbow to wrist and all over the backs of both hands from all the times they had to reinsert the IV.

I had never been admitted to the hospital before, except for childbirth. And I'd certainly never had a medical emergency so far from my family. This was a crash course in life in a new city. Our new friends visited me and brought snacks and pretty lotion, and they watched our kids so Aaron could come see me each day. They sent flowers and prayed for me at church, and what I realized is that a city doesn't become your home because you've been to all the big museums or shows. It becomes your home when your new friends and neighbors come sit next to your hospital bed at Lenox Hill, keeping you company and making you laugh, making you feel not quite so lost and lonely.

I was released from the hospital just before Thanksgiving, which was also our first anniversary of living in the city. Our neighbor Kate hosted the meal, and it was delicious and cozy, and I was acutely grateful for the sweetness of the company and for Kate's hospitality, for this city, for good medical care, and for Jennifer for showing up with an egg sandwich and sitting on my horrible hospital bed with me, and for showing me I wasn't alone.

nineteen

Parenting Ourselves

Most days, I feel like everything I know about parenting could fit on the head of a pin, but in the decade and a half that Aaron and I have been parenting, there are a handful of tricks we keep in our back pocket, cards we play over and over, our works-every-time, tried-and-tested, go-to parenting moves. And like so many things, what's good for our kids is actually really, really good for us grown-ups too. It seems so simple when we tell our kids to do them, but I'm learning, little by little, that what's good for them is good for me too.

Every parent knows that water is a magical mood changer for kids: a shower, a bath with lots of toys, a sprinkler, a splash pad, a garden hose—all of it, mood-changing magic. And the same is true for grown-ups. Things I recommend heartily: a shower in the middle of a bad day, a big glass of water, driving or walking out of your way to get even a glimpse of the water.

Today there was a thunderstorm—a rare, quick-descending storm full of thunder, just like a Midwestern spring storm. The sky darkened in what felt like seconds, not minutes, and I felt that hum of energy and familiarity. A spring storm is as familiar to me as my own face in the mirror—the smell of cement and soil, the crackle of energy as the wind whips up, the sound of the fat raindrops on the sidewalk. It was over as quickly as it started, and now the sun is out again, the sky wiped clean, the leaves glowing and waving back and forth in the breeze. Everything feels gentle and lovely, like a whisper, where before, for those few minutes of the storm, it all felt so severe, pitched, dark. I can feel the reset in my nervous system, calmed and grounded by the storm and the rain, evened out in the post-storm gentleness.

Another one of the core tenets of our parenting is to get outside, run around, work it out with our bodies. My friend Kirsten became a mom of boys before I did, and when Henry was a baby, she told me that boys are like Saint Bernards—sometimes you have to run them. I can't tell you the thousands of times we've pushed our boys out the door—burn some energy, let off some steam, run around the house five times.

Yesterday afternoon we had tentative plans to get together with our neighbors, but as we were texting about plans, we were all ambivalent and tired until Jonathan finally said, "Picnic on the river, leaving in twenty, I'll bring wine."

That's exactly what we did. It was windy and chaotic and the air felt impossibly fresh and everything we owned was in danger of blowing away, but as we walked back afterward, we all thanked Jonathan for getting us outside, for all that air and salt and wind and people watching, for wearing the kids out so that bedtime was a breeze. At every possible opportunity, I try to get outside.

When our kids were little, I never left home without at least three granola bars tucked into my bag, one for each kid and one for Aaron. Life is hard enough without plummeting blood sugar. These days we constantly find ourselves putting out some sort of tide-us-over snack, either for neighbors in the courtyard or friends visiting the city and stopping in to see us for a glass of wine before dinner or a show. My goal is to always be cheeseboard-ready, which means always having at least two cheeses, some salami or prosciutto, crackers, nuts, dried fruits, pickles and olives, jams, or mustards. If you've been to our apartment—or in more recent months our courtyard—you've had a little plate set in front of you: grapes, brie, pistachios or peaches, fresh mozzarella, crusty bread, green olives. Nothing elaborate but always something.

My friend Ian asked me recently what the title of my memoir would be. I thought about it for a minute and decided on *There Will Be Snacks*. I am constitutionally unable to gather a group of people together without just a little something to nibble on. When I think about it, it makes me anxious. *What if someone's hungry? In my home? And I haven't given them a little plate of cheese and pickles?* Our apartment is tiny and never spotless, and it's mostly doors and hallways, but you will always, always be given a snack. It's who I am.

In addition to snacks, sleep is also valued in our house. This past year, ten days after Mac turned eight, Henry turned thirteen. For his party, we played glow-in-the-dark capture the flag and had two friends sleep over after the main party was finished. The next day, Mac was tired—and what began as sleepy-eyed and a little cranky devolved by lunchtime into weepy and combative, and by the time we were getting on the subway to come back home after church and lunch, he was accusatory, basically out of control. His party the week before wasn't as good as Henry's. (Not true.) No one liked him as much as they liked Henry. (Not true.) Henry's gifts were better. (Not true.) His best friend, he was sure, liked Henry better. (Not true.) By the time we got back to the apartment, he was telling us through tears that he'd actually had a pretty bad birthday, that he didn't feel loved or celebrated, and that pretty much everything in his life was bad, and not just accidentally bad but because we made it bad, because we wanted him to be miserable. (Also not true.)

We just let him talk and cry as we brought his blankets and pillow into our bed. We let him talk and cry as we put our arms around him. He fell asleep quickly and slept hard and woke up all back to normal, but the extreme nature of the situation stuck with me the rest of the day. It wasn't like because he was tired he felt things a little more deeply than he usually might; it was like tiredness truly made him think and feel and experience these very dark and sad emotions that were not connected to reality.

Ding ding ding. This is my life. Aaron could barely conceal his laughter, not because Mac was being funny but because it was so uncannily how I experience life when I'm tired—and the bad news for all of us is that I live in such a way that I get myself too tired too often. I've noticed that just like a little kid, on a tough day I need more sleep, and not just physically tough—when I'm wounded or hurt, when the day has been heavy in some way, my body feels it, and my body and spirit both need more rest. I'm not naturally good at rest or listening to my body or, really, any of these life-sustaining practices, but I'm coming to value sleep with each passing year. Sleep is so much more important than we think. I have learned, and now everyone in my house knows, that sometimes Mama just shuts it down and goes to bed at the same time as the kids. And everyone's glad about it.

Since sleep doesn't come easy every time, when I tuck the boys into bed, I tell them they can throw me all their worries, the way kids throw kisses in clenched fists. I catch them, one by one, and tuck each one of them into the pockets of my bathrobe.

They don't tell me what the worries are; they just throw them over to me.

And then, of course, the obvious corollary: when I lie down after tucking them in, I empty my pockets of their worries and mine—*dear God, dear God, dear God.* One of the central jobs of a parent is to hold anything too heavy or hard for their child, and also, that's just exactly what God does for his children, for us. Prayer is grabbing those worries in our fists and throwing them to someone who can hold them for us while we rest.

Another parenting tenet we come back to over and over is to apologize often—and in detail. When I get it wrong, when I snap at one of the boys or fail to listen or lose my cool, I come back to them, apologize, and ask if we can start again. When they're at each other's throats, I call time-out, ask them to apologize to one another, and ask if we can start again. What I love about the quick apology is that we can get right back on track instead of letting the distance between us grow and grow, letting the wound get bigger and bigger. We get it wrong, we make it right, we ask for forgiveness, and we start again. It's important to me that my kids know I get things wrong and that I'm not too prideful to admit it to them. I want them to know that all adults make mistakes, and that part of being in relationship is getting it wrong and then making it right. I'm absolutely crazy about a fullhearted apology, especially these days—it feels like cleaning a wound, gently but thoroughly, carefully wiping out every last shard or splinter, preparing for healing.

Everyone I know has felt the complexity of our world in a thousand different ways recently. Many things have been broken, and one of the greatest gifts we can offer one another is a commitment to caring for ourselves with the same intention and tenderness we use when we care for our kids. Healthy, whole people don't become healthy and whole on accident; it's because they make the small, daily choices that build on each other. These little things won't solve everything, but you might be surprised at how much difference they really can make— for our little ones, of course, but especially for our weary and wounded grown-up selves.

twenty

The Speed of the Soul

Last night before bed, I was reading Rebecca Solnit's *Wanderlust*, a history of walking, and then just at the last minute this morning as Henry and I were leaving to walk him down to school in the West Village, I grabbed my laptop and umbrella. I walked through the West Village, through Washington Square Park, up Fifth, through Madison Square Park, through a vintage furniture store I've been wanting to visit, and then worked for a while in the lobby of a hotel I like.

We all had different things that drew us to New York. Mac had a friend named Harry—the son of old friends of ours now living in New York—and that was all he needed. Henry is a musical theater guy, so Broadway captured him entirely. Aaron loved the progressive culture, great coffee, and the seminary opportunity. And for me—I couldn't wait to walk.

I've had a spotty fitness life at best, but one thing I love anywhere in the world, but especially in cities, is walking. I love to take the long way, I love to watch people, I love the feeling of stretching out hip flexors with long strides and the good-tired feeling in my legs after a long walk. When we first moved, I was in the middle of a sea of grief, and I remember my therapist reminding me that grief is somatic, that it locates itself in our bodies and, therefore, needs to be worked out of our arms and legs and chests with movement. For me, that meant walking.

In addition to grief, before we moved, I was having some serious privacy issues. We lived in a friendly neighborhood in a friendly town. Our kids played Little League and the bus stop was outside our house, but there were days when even just going to the mailbox meant an invitation to conversations I desperately didn't want to have.

Walking through our old neighborhood or our town wasn't an option anymore, and I began to feel a little bit caged. Being in New York, though, the city feels big and anonymous and even though I am surprised at how often we do run into people we know, there's an expansiveness to walking in the city—it's more than big enough for all of us to walk out our grief or fear or anxiety.

There are more than enough blocks and neighborhoods and parks for all our broken hearts and secret wounds and conversations with ourselves, zigzagging the city, our breath ragged, our feet leading us, pushing us forward. When I look back at the first months we spent here in the city, I realize there were a thousand days when a walk in the blinding sun and cold air brought me back to myself, the air in my lungs and the stretch in my hips. Forward motion worked out my grief and my anger and my fear, mile by mile. And it still does.

The spiritual significance of walking is multifaceted—the idea of pilgrimage, of walking in the steps of Jesus or walking the Camino de Santiago in Spain. But also, when I was growing up in the church, we referred to the spiritual aspect of our lives as a "walk." *How's your walk?* we asked each other, as a way of asking about our religious lives or practices. Someone might say, *There's a woman who walks closely with God.*

There are about a million Christian clichés that make me twitch, but this is one I actually love. I love thinking about our spiritual lives or religious experiences as a long walk with someone we love, someone we want to be near and learn from and know deeply. That's what happens when you walk with someone. I like the fact that it's active, something that happens not just in our heads but also in our bodies. I believe religious life happens in our hearts and bodies and not just our brains.

There are times when I wonder about how technology disconnects us more than it connects us, and sometimes I think about air travel: Should we be able to get to the other side of the world in a day? I know that when I look back on my life, the most depleted, disconnected seasons were the ones where I was simply covering too many miles. My body was moving too quickly for my soul and spirit to catch up. But when you're walking, there's no such disconnection.

Maybe walking is the speed of the soul, the exact right pacing for our bodies and spirits and hearts and minds to reconnect, to dwell together again. The soul doesn't thrive in absolute stillness because of what the body holds that needs to be worked out—that grief, that anger. But too high a rate of speed, especially over time, violates the soul, and it's the walking that knits it back together.

There's a lot of research these days about how running pushes the body, how hard it is on the body especially as we age, but walking doesn't—walking feels deeply restorative to me, like it's putting back together the things that have been frayed or broken apart in our lives throughout a day or a week. And it gets my mind moving again, ideas and images and words clicking together like toy railroad tracks, making a path for something beautiful and powerful.

I've known my friend Jennifer for more than ten years—and if it seems to you like most of my friends here in New York are named either Jennifer or Michael, you're exactly right. This Jennifer and I met through mutual friends years ago, and then we worked together on some long-distance projects. And then I moved two blocks away from her apartment in Chelsea and we threw some extremely memorable dinner parties there.

And then during the pandemic, when we couldn't be in each other's apartments and couldn't eat together in a restaurant, we went for walks—so many long walks all over Manhattan. I'd walk east on Twentieth to Fifth, and she'd walk west from her new apartment on Gramercy Park. We'd turn south on Fifth to Washington Square and beyond—sometimes we'd turn on Canal or sometimes we'd go all the way through Tribeca. Sometimes we'd walk back on the West Side Highway along the Hudson, or sometimes we'd loop back through Union Square to walk through the Greenmarket, stopping for apples and tomatillos and fresh bread to take home to my family.

We walked so many miles over the course of that fall. For both of us, it was often the only time we were in person with someone other than our husbands or, in my case, kids. No Zooms, no screens, just breath and steps and city blocks. We walked when it was hot and when it was very cold, and lots of times we walked in the dark, because after daylight savings it got dark before 5:00 p.m. She lost a close family member. I had a serious health scare. We both had work challenges and family tangles, and we were both squarely in the uncertainty of pandemic life—what's next? How do we make plans? Our families think we're crazy—are we crazy? Remember airplanes? Remember dinner parties?

We walked out a thousand frustrations and worries. We walked out our fears and our grief. We covered what seemed like hundreds of miles over those difficult months, and still now when we walk together, we'll swing around a new corner or happen upon a city block we've never walked down before and we'll turn to each other with a sense of delight—there's still so much ground to cover, still so many miles to walk, still so much life and beauty and city to discover. And as we walked, block by block, mile by mile, I started to feel my body and my soul moving at the same speed, in sync and motion and connection.

part three

Cold Moon

twenty-one

A Midlife Move

I used to look at people who moved every couple years with something like sadness—didn't they have a reason to stay? Hadn't they built something solid and substantial? These days I regret the judgment in my eyes. I lived in a town that people stayed in for decades, a town where the kids who grew up there came back and raised their kids there. A town with deep roots, where most of my friends never considered moving out of their school district or living far from their parents.

It was understood that staying put—especially in a town with good schools and grandparents nearby—was a function of good parenting, and everyone wants to be a good parent, of course. There was a sense that living anywhere except the suburb you're already in is a selfish move. Most people seemed to think that there's a time to live in a city, but that usually happens either in college or in your early twenties. Certainly not in midlife.

As it became increasingly clear that a move was the next right step for us, I talked with some families who had moved several times, who believed it was a bonding and memory-making experience, who had gotten used to life without grandparents around the corner and had gotten the hang of new schools, new neighborhoods, new teams. They loved what moving taught them, what it brought out in their marriage, what it brought out in their kids. And all of a sudden, I started to see the smallness of that one perspective—the one that conflates staying put with responsible parenting.

There are a million ways to be a responsible parent. There are a million ways to build a thriving marriage. There are a million ways to lead a meaningful life. But when you've lived only one way for a very long time, the messaging gets really loud, and anything different starts to seem suspect.

In our first year in New York, when we went back to the Midwest for weddings or funerals or family gatherings, we realized that people were concerned about us. *Could it really be true that they actually like it there? Could the kids possibly be happy?*

People were concerned about city life—concerned, I think, that it was terrible and we didn't feel comfortable saying it. It was like they thought maybe we were in a hostage situation—blink twice if you need help! We assured them that, yes, we actually like it. We had visited many times and researched and actually moved to Manhattan on purpose, as people in their forties with two children.

Before we moved here, three people in the same week told me they believed not just New York but this actual apartment would save my life—and it has, one thousand times. This little apartment will always taste like baguettes from La Bergamote, sliced lengthwise and toasted and buttered, eaten while perched on the stool in the corner of the kitchen, looking out the window.

Wherever life takes us, I'll always remember the first morning sounds of Twenty-First Street, and the last look of the Empire State Building at the end of the day. The soft light of the seminary chapel—the lights always on, the doors always open. The sound of helicopters, the familiar path down Ninth and Greenwich to Henry's school.

I believed I would live in my hometown forever, and that my parents and brother and best friends and in-laws would all do the same. We'd drive our roots down in that town so deep we'd be safe forever. Everything in life that we would experience or see, we would see from that vantage point—the center of the world.

I was cleaning out my closet recently and realized that almost every T-shirt, sweatshirt, and hat I own references Chicago or the Midwest or Michigan. For so many years, I believed in the idea of place as identity. I don't know about that anymore. I love living in New York, and at the same time, moving here showed me I could live happily in so many places, and that where I live doesn't dictate who I am. I could live in Madison or Houston or the Florida Keys and I'd still be me— still a bookworm who reads cookbooks like novels and eats cold pizza for breakfast and has a thing for striped shirts.

Moving doesn't change who we are, even though sometimes we wish it would. But it does change our vantage point on the world. It swivels us around to see things in ways we've never seen them before. It shakes loose our assumptions and brings us back around to humility and curiosity as we learn a new world, a new rhythm and map and set of customs and agreements, and all that work is good work, keeping us adaptable and open.

I still have more Midwest-themed clothing than I do NYC gear, but sometimes, just for fun, I wear my Saugatuck shirt with my Yankees hat, a little nod to how the map of my heart is unfolding to include a new city.

twenty-two

Put Yourself in the Path

For years, when I've taught writing workshops or been interviewed on the topic of creativity, someone inevitably asks about "being inspired"—or staying inspired or getting inspired—and I get so excited. I jump up on my little soapbox and tell them what I know about inspiration, that there's a myth that it's mercurial and wispy, that it's floaty and unpredictable and you just cross your fingers and hope it lands on you at the right time. "Not true!" I tell them. Inspiration is my responsibility. Inspiration is part of the job description. It doesn't strike like lightning. I lay myself open to receive it.

You can't manhandle it or make demands of it, but you can put yourself in the path of it. You make yourself available to it. It's my job as a writer to live in such a way that every time I sit down to write, I'm inspired, not in the moment necessarily, but in my life, as a way of life. What this means is that it's my job, literally, to go to art galleries and read poetry and go for walks and spend time with interesting people. It's part of my work to read widely and learn new things and be curious and ask questions and wonder and doodle and dream, because living inspired is a requirement for rich creative work.

You can't watch bad television and endlessly scroll Twitter and expect great things to show up on the page. It's your responsibility as a creative person to actively put yourself in the path of inspiration. I learned some of this out of practical necessity. When I was writing my first book, I had a newborn. I did not have the luxury of lollygagging around, waiting for inspiration to strike. The baby ate every three hours, and so I wrote like a madwoman for two hours and fifty-seven minutes, and then I ran two blocks, unhooking my nursing bra as I flew through the door, back to the babysitter and the baby. That was great training for me, useful in my work in a thousand ways since.

And now I'm realizing, in yet another way, that I have expected joy and faith and hope to rise within me the way they have in other seasons. Where are they? What are they waiting for? What I'm learning is that in the same way we put ourselves in the path of inspiration, we also put ourselves in the path of joy, and sometimes, frankly, it takes a little muscle.

I no longer wait for joy to rise up unbidden. I put myself in her path every chance I get, and extending myself in that direction delivers me to gratitude, to hope, to a cascade of things that tumble out after joy but don't show up without a little effort on our part.

One morning, just after we moved, when even easy things still felt chaotic and complicated, I did not wake up joyful. I felt groggy and annoyed, and one of my sons needed to be asked seventeen times to get in the shower and the other (1) asked me to fill out a school form right as he was walking out the door, (2) scolded me for not doing it sooner, and (3) then forgot the dumb form anyway—after I rushed to do it, after he scolded me about it.

But then something extraordinary happened. It was my day

to walk Mac and our neighbors' kids to school, and on my way to drop them off, I saw eight familiar, kind faces. That might not seem like much, but if you consider that when we moved here, I knew only nine people total, eight people to say good morning to felt really good.

It gets better. After I dropped them off, I went on to Trader Joe's, which is my happy place, and my favorite cashier, Medley, and I rocked out to Paula Abdul's "Straight Up" as he rang me up—we both knew absolutely every word. Also, I bought an enormous tray of fresh figs. I didn't really even know what to do with them, but just seeing them on the windowsill made me happy. And then one more moment of victory: I bought just enough to fit in the four totes I'd brought. That might seem like an extremely small cause for joy, unless you know how many times I had bought way too much and had to text Aaron from Twenty-First Street and beg him to come and help me get everything home.

One of my goals is to be a person who is easily delighted, who can find great cause for celebration in a fig or a familiar face. If you need fireworks and perfection in order to crack a smile, you're going to be disappointed over and over when life fails to be spectacular on command. I want to live with an extremely low bar for delight. It takes almost nothing at all—a good song, a ripe piece of fruit, a perfectly packed tote.

You are allowed to love tiny, daily, ordinary moments in your life. You're allowed to feel wild joy for the simplest and smallest of reasons. You're allowed to be unreasonably delighted by spicy pickles or a perfect apple or a joke your teen tells you. You're allowed to be bewitched by your partner, even after all these years, to yearn to be close to him, to bury your face in his neck. You're allowed to feel joy for almost no reason, except that you walked by the candle that your mother sent you and even when it's not lit, just seeing it there on the hutch makes you happy. You're allowed to hold memories in your mind and play them over and over like an old-fashioned slideshow—*click, click, click*.

My mom loves a good mug, satisfyingly heavy, and my mother-in-law loves cozy slippers and marshmallows. I love the tree right outside the kitchen window, the smell of raisin toast, the way Mac comes in most mornings, sleepy and warm, for a quick snuggle.

I'm learning to choose myself instead of giving the best of myself to people and relationships and institutions. Loyalty to myself. Belonging to myself. Looking for joy just for myself. I need a disproportionate amount of care right now, and the one who is responsible for that care is me. I can't assume that someone else will do it; it's my responsibility to create a rhythm for my life that nurtures me, that brings me joy, that allows me to flourish, even given the weight of things I'm carrying.

I'm learning to put myself in the path of joy and beauty. I'm making my life small and simple. I'm building a shelter for myself—writing, walking, reading, cooking. Self-compassion, simplicity, joy, rest.

The other morning, I heard a noise in the normally quiet courtyard—two women in their black priestly robes were yelling, almost gleefully. One was teaching the other how to swing the incense, but things were definitely getting a little out of hand—one was swinging wildly, and the other was dodging the smoky globe, both swirling and twirling like children, all the while whooping and laughing loudly. I watched it like a movie and realized at a certain point that tears were running down my cheeks. There it was—joy, irreverence, play. I got to peek into an unguarded moment of freedom and silliness, and I needed it so badly.

twenty-three

The New York Way

Our family has a few core values, timeless and defining. But we also have values for a season—sort of a guiding principle or idea to help us navigate through a particular moment. As we were moving from the Midwest to Manhattan, one of our values was to ask, "What's the New York way?"

In any new situation, when we didn't know what to do, we asked ourselves, *What's the New York way to do this?* We knew it would be easy, especially when we were nervous or stressed, to want to go back to how things were, to cling to the past, to demand that this big city be just like our quiet suburb. And so we told ourselves, *We aren't trying to live in New York as though it's the exact same place we came from*. We wanted to always be asking the question: What's the New York way to do this or that?

And two weeks after we arrived, we had an opportunity to live into that value and let it guide our choices in a very specific way.

In the Midwest, or at least where we used to live, if you're starting your kids in a new school, they do a very long, very involved onboarding process—the child, the parents, the principal, the guidance counselor, all the teachers. There are evening meetings and tours and visits and buddies assigned to your child. And it's very relational. You talk about your child, but also where you live and where you went to school and if you have any mutual friends and what you're doing for the holidays.

And then we moved to New York, and they told us which school we were zoned for. They said to pick a day to bring proof of address and a birth certificate, and the kids would start the next day.

So we show up with our first grader, Mac. It's December. We have our forms, and the parent coordinator looks at them and says, "Hmm. Our birthday cutoffs are different here, and other kids born in his same month and year are in second grade." And I was like, "That's interesting, but he's only been in first grade for three months . . ."

Just then a class walks by and the parent coordinator says to the students, "Hey, what grade are you in? Are you first graders?"

He continued, "Mac, you're taller than they are. Here—can you read this book? And this one?" And then he starts asking Mac questions: "How do you feel about moving?" "What do you like about living in New York so far?" And Mac reads the books and tells him he really likes Shake Shack and how he and his brother have new bunk beds.

The parent coordinator turns to us and says, "I'm recommending we start him in second grade. His birthday puts him right in the right age range, he's tall, and judging by the reading assessment and social/emotional assessment I just gave him, he's ready for second grade. Tomorrow."

In our hometown this would have taken six weeks. We would know each other's life stories. There would be specialists and documents. And in that moment, I really missed that methodical, conversational, long and detailed and extremely relational process.

But we went back to our core question: What's the New York way?

So we took a deep breath, and Mac started second grade the next day—and he's thriving. I'm really grateful for that parent coordinator because he showed us the New York way.

Last night, a friend's all-time favorite jazz trio was playing at the Village Vanguard at 10:30 p.m. and a bunch of great people were going. At first we thought to ourselves, *We don't go anywhere at 10:30 on a Wednesday night!* But then we stopped ourselves and said, "Well, maybe our old selves mostly didn't, but maybe our New York selves do?"

And so we went, and of course we loved it. A date with my favorite person and people we enjoy so much, a historic venue, pizza at midnight on Bleecker, a beautiful walk home through the West Village—on a school night! Being in a new place has opened us up, shaken off patterns and assumptions, created space to make things up again—and I'm so happy about it.

twenty-four

Grief Is a Kitten

The healthiest, most wholehearted people I know are the ones who have suffered, who have lost, who have wrestled, who have pushed back up to the surface. I thought that getting fired from a job I loved was my reckoning—the thing that would break my addiction to security and control. It did and it didn't. I thought that our interminable stretch of miscarriages and infertility would tenderize me in deep ways, forge in me a deep peace, even in suffering. It did and it didn't.

You may be clinging to the past because it feels familiar and safe. But it's gone, and you can't go back. I'm sorry. I know. I tried too.

You may be heartbroken and lonely because the people you thought you'd walk through all your life with have walked away from you. I'm sorry. I know.

You have to fight your way back up. There's no other option. I'm sorry about that too. You don't have the choice you think you have—I know, because I wanted to give up and choose weakness about a thousand times, conservatively.

When we've experienced a great loss, often we say we're sad—we're grieving or mourning—but what bubbles out of us like a volcano is anger: hot, volatile, explosive anger. Anger is active, powerful; it buoys us along and gives us something to do and focus on and sharpen. Anger makes us feel like we're in control again, because loss is, at its core, loss of control, or the myth of it anyway—I couldn't keep that person alive. I couldn't make them stay. I couldn't fix our problems. I couldn't save whatever it is that was broken.

Grief involves the terrifying sense of being out of control, and anger gives us back the feeling of control—it's not accurate but it's familiar, and it feels a whole lot better than the tenderness and emptiness of sadness. If anger is active and powerful, grief and sadness are tender, vulnerable. Anger puts us back in the power position, while grief lays us bare, like letting ourselves lie down on a sidewalk, knowing we could get stepped on, crushed. Grief gives up the pretense of control. It's lonely and quiet and submitted to the enormity of what has been lost, like being underwater. For most of us, anger is more familiar—and much safer.

A question though: If you take a long look at your anger, might there be grief underneath it, like a small child hiding behind a warrior? When it comes down to it, it takes more bravery to be sad than to be angry, but anger is a way of self-protecting—an armor we sometimes choose when sadness feels too scary.

I have felt so much anger the last couple years, and it's mostly anger that someone else has changed my life—I've had to make choices according to a reality that's not of my choosing . . . and it certainly speaks to the enormous privilege of my life that this is a foreign feeling to me. Because of my privilege, I've been able to make my own choices, or the choices that have been made for me have benefited me tremendously. Until now.

So the anger manifests itself as fury because I feel out of control, but if I sit with the anger for a little while, if I let it teach me, if I get down on the floor with it the way you would a suspicious cat, over time the cat reveals itself to be not a lion but a kitten—brokenhearted, fragile, small. I find my fragile grief, masquerading as powerful anger. I'm sad that this is a plot point I have to incorporate into the story of my life. That's the heart of it. I don't want this part. I want to stick my fingers in my ears like a child. I want to lock the door against it. *You can't be a part of my story.*

Under the anger, there's the soft belly of grief. Beautiful things have been broken, like the snapping of a branch. My heart believes in forgiveness—indeed, forgiveness has become increasingly central to my own spiritual practice and health.

One way you realize you're healing: For a while, what you've suffered is the biggest thing you can imagine. In your pain and suffering, you twist reality around your own wound and you see the whole world through the lens of your pain. For a time, what you're facing really is the biggest, ugliest, cruelest thing that anyone could ever be allowed to experience. And then over time, as you fight to heal, as you move forward, one foot in front of the other over and over again, you begin once again to see other people's losses as weighty and real—as real, even, as what you've lost.

This is good. This is healing. Your pain is being rightsized— still real and still tender and still awful, but not the biggest, hardest thing in all the world. You start to have the emotional energy to offer to other people in empathy, seeing what they're carrying instead of hoarding up all your resources for the cavern of your own loss.

Empathy is a sister to compassion. It's a willing cracking open of the heart, over and over, an intentional tenderness of spirit. It takes discipline and bravery to practice empathy—it's far easier to demonize the other when we focus on the differences and the distances, when we separate people into us versus them.

Empathy is what allows us to be gracious with our kids in those quarantine moments when they're driving us up every wall—because they didn't choose this either, because their lives have been upended too, because they're lonely and scared too.

Empathy is when white people listen to the stories and experiences of their Black friends—without defensiveness, without trying to distance or absolve themselves from white supremacy or systemic racism.

Empathy is choosing to see what connects us all—our common humanity. Our common resolve as well as our common fragility, our common grief and terror and exhaustion as well as our common hope and joy and delight.

Empathy is when we see another person's needs and longings as clearly as we see our own, when we feel another person's wounds and scars as if they were wounds and scars on our very own body, our very own skin. Empathy stitches us together when a thousand loud things act as seam rippers, shredding the fabric of our connectedness. Empathy simply picks up a needle and begins stitching again—together, together, together.

When I read the Bible, I read story after story of love, of redemption, of subverting the status quo in order to love more deeply and powerfully. Jesus is a surprising and almost shocking person—one who breaks boundaries and rules in order to love people who haven't been loved by the world around them. That's what it means to be a Christian—to model your life after Jesus, the one who embodies love. Jesus did not preserve boundaries and traditions at the expense of humans. He valued humans at the expense of previously held boundaries and traditions. Christlikeness is, at its core, about love—a brave, muscular, boundary-breaking love for all people, a commitment to human thriving on every level. I believe that calling myself a Christian means living up to Christ's example of brave, sometimes shocking love.

twenty-five

On Prayer

Thomas Keller, one of my favorite chefs, has a way of thinking about recipes that I just love. He says the first time you use a recipe, do it exactly as written. Follow every direction, every measurement. That way, you taste what the recipe writer or the chef had in mind exactly. Then the next time, you rewrite the recipe in your own words as simply as possible—you're moving from their language to your language. Once you've rewritten the recipe your way, make the dish according to your new recipe. The third time, make it only from memory, and make at least one change—switch out a vegetable, change a spice— something to make it different from the original. Keller says that after you've made it for the third time, the recipe is yours. You've internalized it. It's not a recipe in a cookbook; it's in you, it's part of you.

Several weeks ago, I started thinking about prayer in this way. While I've learned and unlearned many aspects of my faith perspective and practice over the years, prayer has remained central. It's always been a through line of my life as a Christian, but lately prayer has become a lifeline.

Prayer is a way to entrust the people we love to God, especially when things feel out of our control. I've felt that out-of-control feeling so acutely this last year—I think all of us have.

Prayer is acknowledging that we are not in control—but that someone is. There is a God who holds us, who holds it all, who is trustworthy and powerful, and who is more than strong enough to hold the enormity of our fear and worry.

In the New Testament, Jesus prays for his disciples, the group of people he loves, about four specific things: union, protection, joy, and sanctification. I wanted to pray for the people I love in the same way, so I tried doing it like one of Keller's recipes.

The first couple times I did it, I used the specific form Jesus did—union, protection, joy, and sanctification—and wrote out my prayers so I could be specific and detailed. It was very moving to pray for each of our kids, to entrust them to God's care. I mean, I pray for my kids in general, but the pattern and the specificity were especially meaningful. I wrote about things that would bring joy to Mac, specific situations in which I want Henry to be protected from any harm. I prayed for Aaron, that he would have a strong sense of connection and support from me and from our community.

The next couple times, I prayed while I was walking in the city—union, protection, joy, sanctification. After that, I started using my own words that get at the same things—instead of union, support; instead of protection, blessing; instead of joy, delight; instead of sanctification, Christlikeness.

I noticed that I felt more connected throughout the day to those I was praying for. I felt more aware of my kids' safety instead of taking it for granted. I noticed when Aaron said something about a friendship he appreciated or something that brought him joy in the course of a day. I became more attuned to them, to their lives and spirits and desires and frustrations, and I prayed for those things too. Praying for the people I love was helping me love them in deeper ways—it was cyclical in a way. More prayer yielded more attentiveness to their lives, which inspired me toward more prayer, and so on.

I was making the prayer my own, in my own words and rhythms and practices. I prayed it in the middle of the night when I couldn't sleep. I prayed it while I was making dinner—as I chopped vegetables, I prayed those four words for the people I love.

After that, instead of praying in words and sentences, I closed my eyes and imagined a snapshot of each thing. For protection, I pictured Mac safe in our home. For joy, I imagined Aaron laughing at something one of our kids says—true delight on his face. For sanctification, I pictured Henry praying at bedtime.

I found that this way of praying, this pattern, these four words, were starting to feel natural, like something that was a part of me, something I embodied, not something I memorized or performed.

In addition to praying for my family, I also chose to pray for a particular friend—our friendship has been badly broken, and that brokenness has caused me so much pain. This friend has been a part of my life for a long time, someone I respect, someone I've learned so much from. A difficult situation came between us, and it brought out the worst in both of us.

I've tried to fix it but can't. And living with a broken relationship to someone I care about so much bothers me every day. It's like having a splinter in your heel that you feel with every step. You never forget. You're always carrying the weight of this broken relationship. And so I began to pray for them. What I love about this pattern of prayer is that it isn't a free-for-all, and it can't be turned into a laundry list of what I think is right. *Dear God, please help this person to see the error of their ways. Dear God, please open their eyes. Dear God, please give me patience to deal with the mess they've made . . .*

I didn't do that. I prayed for union, that my friend will be connected and supported and that at some point I'll be a part of that with them again. I prayed for protection—that they will be kept safe, body, spirit, heart. That nothing will cause them pain—not even me. I prayed for joy. I asked God to bring joy into their life every day—I thought about some things that they love, experiences or moments that I know would be joyful for them, and even though I won't be a part of them, I asked God to bring those moments and experiences into their life. And then I prayed for their sanctification—that they will be brave and kind and generous, growing in tenderness and love for others and being willing to stand up for what's right.

I prayed every day for this person. I wish I could tell you that while I was praying for them, the phone rang and the silence between us was broken. Or that I opened my eyes, pushed away from my desk, and ran to catch a flight to show up on their doorstep. Maybe one of those things is coming. Maybe not. I don't know.

The more life I live, the more certain I am that movie moments only happen in the movies, but I also know that if things are going to be repaired between my friend and me, it's only going to happen because we're both humble and tender enough to drop our defenses, lay down our anger, and connect across the distance we've created.

After a couple of weeks of praying for my friend like this every day—with words, with imagination, with love—God has not yet healed the relationship, but he has shifted my heart in a way that makes me believe nearly anything can happen.

Prayer is like yoga for our insides. My number one favorite kind of yoga is the kind that's mostly breathing and lying down. But my second favorite kind is when you're in a pose that's really demanding, and for just a few seconds you trust your body and you trust your breath and your body becomes able in that moment to do things it wasn't able to do before. It's an amazing feeling.

This is the sacred, interior version of that. When we pray for people with whom we have difficult or painful relationships, God works lovingly and powerfully inside us, rebuilding and restoring us, shaping us into the kind of people who forgive and repair and give second chances—the kind of people we all want to be but can't always get there on our own. This is what prayer can do. This is what God can do.

Try praying every single day for a handful of people you love. Start with the four words, and then make it your own—your own words, your own rhythm, your own embodied and personal way of entrusting your family and friends to God through prayer, the way Jesus entrusted his disciples to his Father through prayer.

And now here's a challenge: include someone with whom you have a complicated or broken relationship. I'm not an expert in prayer or friendship or anything, but I do know that just a couple weeks of this way of praying has loosened something inside me that has been clenched like a fist for a long time. Prayer changes us—it's God's sacred tool, able to transform and rebuild us from the inside out, day by day, breath by breath, prayer by prayer.

twenty-six

Delete/Unfollow/ Unsubscribe

For many years, I've said that technology is neutral, that by design it's not inherently good or bad, but we have to decide how to engage with it. I still believe that's true about the actual capacity of the internet. But I don't think that's true about social media.

As the number of people connecting with my social media grew, things began to feel very loud. I'm not at all sure we're meant to be interacting with and handling the feelings of so many people. I'm an empath, a person who feels the feelings and emotions of the people around her quite acutely. Carrying the emotional weight of too many people—too many feelings and desires and expectations—flattens me. I want, genuinely, to meet the needs and expectations of all these people, but it's mathematically impossible, so I end up exhausted and resentful.

The sheer volume of voices is too much for most of us, if we're honest. It's like standing in the center of a packed stadium every single day and expecting the constant noise and jostling not to take their toll on your spirit.

For me, the hardest part isn't the temptation to keep track

of the amount of likes and comments; it's about how quickly a stranger can show up in my life and, more than that, why I keep letting them. If strangers kept coming to my door, asking to be let into my actual house to tell me everything they ever thought about me and my life and my family, I would move. Why have I allowed strangers into my mental living room and my mind and my heart?

I've been putting more and more boundaries on my social media use. Some weeks I've been checking in on it only on the weekends, and I find that I love the days I spend without it. For too many years in my life, there were too many voices, too many opinions, too much screaming and experting and lecturing, and I'm reveling in the newfound silence that these breaks have yielded. And I've become much more conscious of the dangers of social media, realizing that over time we begin to internalize the cruelty and abuse we encounter there.

I didn't grasp it at the time, but little by little, I began to believe the voices of strangers. I stopped believing it was okay for me to draw boundaries to protect myself. I took it, and I took it, and I took it. I had been fed a steady diet of shame and cruelty, without protection, without safety, without the ability to say, "You can't speak to me like this. You're breaking me."

For years, I didn't delete, block, mute, report nearly soon enough. I didn't reach out soon enough. I didn't put boundaries around my own social media use soon enough. And I regret those things so deeply because ultimately I kept reexposing myself to pain and cruelty when I should have been protecting myself. I thought I was being tough, but really I was being unsafe and unwise. Cruelty and shame break us over time, and part of growth is choosing what we will and will no longer allow into our lives.

When you write about someone who has a public voice,

it's easy to think of that person as less than human. It's easy to think of all the things you think they have—power or privilege or money or ease—and then trick yourself into believing they're not vulnerable to your cruelty. You're David and they're Goliath. You're the underdog and they're the problem.

That's not true, though, and we've seen over and over in recent years the very serious pain that people experience via social media. I've been wounded deeply as I've read cruel and abusive words that people have written about me and to me on social media, and for a long time, I allowed it. I felt like I had to for some reason—like because I had the tremendous privilege of being heard, I had to be willing to hear everything else. I don't think that anymore.

It's healthy and right to protect ourselves from cruelty. I listen closely to people who have earned my trust, and I intentionally limit the number of voices who get to tell me who I am. The people who get to tell me who I am are the ones who have invested in me, who know me, who walk with me and see the everyday me. We've created a system where people who know nothing about us can broadcast their take on us, and if you've ever been on the receiving end of that, you know it can do a surprising amount of damage.

I'm consciously creating more silence in my life. I'm reading more and more books and fewer and fewer tweets. I think we're going to look back at this hot-take outrage machine and grieve what we lost along the way: Sober-mindedness. Willingness to let a story unfold over time. Wisdom. Perspective. Kindness toward our fellow humans.

I'm not going to spend my life hovering around the internet, weighing in on everything in real time. I'm not going to open my life and my heart to thousands of strangers and carry the weight of their opinions around with me everywhere I go. I'm not sure we yet understand the toll these innocuous-seeming little websites are taking on our hearts and spirits. But I'm starting to understand it for my own life.

I'm deleting and unfollowing and unsubscribing left and right these days for all sorts of reasons. I don't have the capacity for snark or sarcasm that I used to. I don't want to be yelled at or shamed or talked down to. I don't have an unlimited capacity for outrage. I tend to follow people who seem to have a sense of groundedness, of commitment to the long game, of wisdom that accompanies their passion.

The amount of time most of us are spending scrolling through other people's lives and opinions is staggering— choose wisely whose voices you're allowing into your life, because I know from experience that after a while, they become the voices not just on your screen but in your head.

Put down your phone. Delete your apps. Or even just move your social media a few screens back on your phone. I make sure I can text and read a book on the front screen of my phone and that I have to swipe several times to get to social apps, which means when I pick up my phone out of habit, texting and reading—things I want to do more of—are right there and easy to use, and social apps take a few extra steps. Even little things like that help me. Admit when your most tender or vulnerable times are, and discipline yourself not to open yourself up to social media in those moments. For me, that's when I'm in bed. On the one hand, I'm sleepy and cozy and I want to scroll through and see what my friends' cute kids are up to. On the other hand, why on earth would I allow thousands of strangers' opinions to visit me while I'm in my pajamas? It's insane what we're allowing into our lives.

This may sound extreme, but especially when I was in a season during which I felt extra exposed or was experiencing more cruelty than usual, I checked social media only while dressed at my desk, like a professional grown-up woman. I couldn't afford to have someone's abuse reach through my phone while I was absentmindedly scrolling in bed, so I had to make new habits, and they've saved me.

You decide who you allow into your life. Unfollow a whole slew of people. Make your world really quiet sometimes, especially when things are hard or when you have a difficult decision to make. Follow people you want to be like—because that's what happens, for better and for worse. If you curate a list of compassionate, kind people, you'll bend toward kindness; if you curate a list of snark, you'll start to hear it in your own voice. If everyone you follow is buying something or selling something, you'll find that this wanting itch will get extra itchy over time.

There's a proverb that reads, "Guard your heart, for everything you do flows from it" (Proverbs 4:23). Anyone who went to Christian youth group knows this proverb mostly in a dating context, but when I think about what it means to guard my heart these days, I think about what I'm allowing in and what I'm not allowing in. I want more kindness, more love, more compassion. I can't allow in cruelty or meanness or snark. Because our hearts are the wellspring, the center from which everything else flows, and it's up to each of us to tend to our heart and protect it.

For a long time, I wanted people on social media to change—to be less cruel, to be decent, to be fair, to tell the truth. That would be lovely. But I'm not waiting around for that. I'm deciding who gets to enter my spaces, my heart, my mind, my living room, because I'm responsible for those places, no one else. I'm responsible to protect my mind, my heart, my family. I can't change anyone else. I can't make them kinder or fairer or more measured or less cruel. But I get to decide which voices I listen to and which I don't, and when to put down my phone and protect my own life.

twenty-seven

On Having a Body

This morning, we visited a church in our neighborhood where our friend Christine is the priest. It's a gorgeous old stone building with a beautiful clock tower, and as Aaron and I walked over, the breeze was mild and the air was sweet. We sang and prayed and passed the peace, and Christine preached on the passage from Ephesians about how we are all parts of the same body, united as one and each necessary to the whole, each one of us interconnected with one another.

Her eyes glistened with tears as she explained that this has been a season of struggle for her, and that she doesn't always know how much of her own emotional life she should share from the pulpit. She talked about feeling the pressure to be a different kind of priest—more male, more white, more alpha. And then she said, "But I've decided that what God is asking of me—and what he's asking of all of us—is for each of us to show up to the body of Christ as our own selves, whatever that means—whatever gifts, whatever weaknesses, whatever dreams, whatever callings."

I realized that my eyes were full of tears too, and I was caught off guard a little bit by the wave of emotion that her words and her vulnerability triggered in me. I began to scribble notes to myself on a little pad of paper I always keep in my purse. What does it mean to show up as deeply myself right now? What does it mean to give my whole self to my community instead of only the parts that feel acceptable and easy?

Christine kept coming back to the body—to the scriptural image of the body, all the parts working together, the embodied nature of faith and life. This is, to be honest, hard for me in general, but especially hard right now. There's a funny dichotomy in me. In most areas, I'm a flesh-and-bone, blood-and-guts person. I love texture and fragrance and getting my hands dirty. I love walking barefoot and I'm a hugger and a snuggler and I believe wholeheartedly in the sense-drenched, embodied way of living in and experiencing the world. I want to taste it all, feel it all, hold it all in my hands.

And yet I have struggled and am struggling with having a body—particularly a middle-aged body, a sick body, a body that doesn't look or feel like it used to. I was so aware, today in church, of the ways my body these days feels unruly and foreign and wrong, and I was looking at everyone else with curiosity. Did you all just wake up and feel normal and at peace with your body? Did any of you feel at war, like a foreigner on foreign soil, like an enemy?

I love the physical, embodied world until it comes to my own body. There are times when I find myself thinking, *I hate having a face. I hate having a body. I love this world and I hate having to walk around in it with this body, this sick and unruly and unpredictable body.* I was half joking with a friend earlier this spring when I said, "I'm just so sorry that you have to eat dinner with my arms."

I know better than this. Of course I do. I know that it's with my arms that I hold my children. I know that relative health is nothing to take for granted. I know that it's downright offensive to be consumed with one's upper arms—the height of privilege.

I know I wanted to be done with all this years ago, and the fact that I'm nearing my forty-fifth birthday and still struggling with my relationship to my body after all these years makes me feel something like despair.

And yet. One thing I do sometimes when I'm stuck within my own worst tangles is to try to talk to myself like I would talk to someone I love. If one of my best friends came to my house and sat on my sofa with me and said, "It's so painful to me that I'm going on basically my fortieth year of struggling to live well in my body," what would I say to her?

I'd start by holding her hand if she'd allow me. I'd let the warmth of my fingers spread to her fingers, and I'd hold on with the same gentle kind of pressure we use when we hold babies close to help them fall asleep, that reassuring pressure that says, *You are held. Your nervous system can unclench, just for a minute. You can allow yourself to go off high alert—I'll take this shift.*

I'd say to my friend, "This is hard. I'm sorry. And it isn't just you." When I'm spinning out, I always think I'm the only one—I see people in all sorts of bodies, and I just assume they're all reveling in their own skin, whatever their height or weight or age or limitation. I think, *Oh, it must be so nice to just swan down the street loving how it feels to be in your body right now.* Why do I assume that's what everyone else is experiencing?

We live in a culture that is obsessed with impossible beauty and weight standards, especially for women. Why on earth would I assume that most of the women around me are sailing through it, and I'm the only one who's not? Why would I assume that everyone else feels like hot stuff, and I'm the only one who doesn't? Billions of dollars are spent every year making sure that's not the case, that we're dissatisfied enough with our appearance and our faces and our skin and our bodies that we need everything they tell us we need, and I'm not immune to that.

There are things that come relatively naturally to me. I almost never doubt my intelligence or my ability to speak or write in a reasonably effective way. I was raised by parents who affirmed my intellectual capacities—that's not something I wonder about day to day. But I'm as cracked up as anyone I know when it comes to living peaceably in my own skin and body. I've been self-conscious about my appearance since my earliest conscious memories, and still to this day, I have to push myself to just walk away from the mirror and out the door because if I stay in front of the mirror too long, I'll never go anywhere.

Living in New York has been freeing in ways I didn't anticipate. Lots of times, big cities feel so cosmopolitan and competitive and flashy, and sometimes they push all my body-shame buttons, but New York has made everything easier for me. Some of it is the diversity in every way. There are so many different kinds of bodies—old and young and short and tall—and there are so many ways to be fashionable or pretty or cool.

You can have nails three inches long, elaborately painted, like the woman who works at the bookstore near us. Or you can have rainbow hair or be completely bald or wear sequins to breakfast or your pajamas in Central Park, and it's all exciting and lovely. There are old men who wear three-piece suits and fancy hats to the French bakery on our corner, and also gaggles of young women in crop tops and enormous sneakers. The sheer variety of it is freeing, like we're not all supposed to look the same, like there's not one ideal shape or age or look or style. That helps me so much.

But still. This is the truth about me right now. There have

been moments—and I dearly hope there are moments again—when I have felt happy in my own skin, owning every inch of the body that has carried me through life. I hope there are days when I can even just forget about it for a little while. But these are not those days.

There are days when I can't draw a full breath. There are nights when I wake up drenched over and over. There are times when I make my way up the three flights to our apartment and stand in the kitchen, doubled over, hoping not to vomit.

I can see the exhaustion in my eyes, and my kids have begun remarking quite often that the backs of my hands are becoming "grandma hands." Nothing fits right. Nothing feels right. I'm reaching for floor-length dresses, fighting the urge to stay home, forcing myself to show up and not apologize that I brought along with me a body I don't love living in right now.

I hate that that's true. I wanted to have this nailed. I wanted to leave this part of my life firmly in the past. But that's not how it is. Here we are again.

I guess I still haven't learned this one yet.

twenty-eight
North Fork

In the fall, my friends Kate and Kyndi and I packed up a rental car and drove to a little house on the North Fork of Long Island. We arrived at the little cottage later than we'd planned, after dark, with just enough time to unload the rental car and put our bags in our room before our dinner reservation at The Halyard in Greenport.

When we got there, it looked like an old motor lodge or summer camp that had been recently redone, glossy white paint over the wide plank floors, the stone fireplace, and the ceiling beams.

We knew we were nearish to the water, but the sky was dark. We asked our server how to get to the water, and she definitely thought we were crazy, but she did show us the door at one end of the large white room. We pushed the door against the wind and gasped—we were right there, right on the water, just a few feet from the rocks and swirling surf, that briny smell and roaring crash. Just as quickly we went back inside where it was silent and warm, but we knew the sea was still there, wild and loud right on the other side of the glass, ominous and beautiful and dark.

We ordered biscuits and a flatbread with whipped ricotta and honey and truffles, cavatappi Bolognese, and fish and chips that were crispy and salty and light with a sauce gribiche I wanted to drink.

Kate asked me how the writing was going, and the tears came before I could even answer. And I can feel, still now, all the shame and embarrassment of crying over what was supposed to be a sweet getaway dinner, but also I know I needed it, needed to cry, needed to be heard, needed their advice and assurance.

Throughout this fall, I was learning over and over, in so many ways, about chronic pain, about living in a broken body and with a broken spirit. I was learning—slowly, begrudgingly—to let people who loved me enter into it, to let myself feel things and let people who loved me feel them too.

That night on the North Fork, I did just that, accidentally. I hated it so much and I was thoroughly mortified. They didn't give me a plan or magically solve it; they just held it with me, and I woke up in the morning with more clarity and hope than I'd had in months.

The next day, we walked on the beach—a severe, wind-whipping winter beach, one of my favorite things on earth. The waves were roaring so loudly we couldn't hear each other, so we just walked in silence, trying not to get our boots wet, trying not to let our hats and scarves get blown away in the swirling cold wind. I picked up three white stones and tucked them in my pocket.

When we got back to the city, I stacked them one on top of the other on the bookcase by my desk, a little cairn of sorts, a reminder that I wasn't alone, even when the wind and the waves were roaring.

twenty-nine

Pink Folder

On my desk in the corner of our bedroom I have a file box for all my "active" files—I keep all the long-term file boxes on the top shelf of our kitchen pantry, so the ones on my desk are just the ones I reach for every day—the boys' school forms, bills to pay, upcoming work events. I labeled a bright pink folder "Shauna Health" and stuffed it with referrals and hospital bills and insurance forms.

In all the insanity of the hospital stay, I had nearly forgotten that weird conversation with my ob-gyn about my tiny, shrunken ovaries, but I eventually made myself schedule a follow-up. After I had blood work done, I grabbed my health folder and headed back to her office as she explained the results of my blood work—full menopause, about ten years early.

My hormone levels suggested I was quite far along in the process, and she was surprised I was even still bleeding. She suggested an herbal supplement to try for three months and then told me to come back if I needed more support.

I walked home through the flower district, weaving in and out of the potted plants that lined the sidewalks. I went over our short conversation in my mind, connecting some dots I'd been wondering about for a long time. I remembered that when I was thirty-nine, I said to a good friend that my body had lost its mind. At that point, I thought it was stress-related, and probably some of it was, but looking back, was menopause part of it too? How much of the chronic and confusing pain and sickness I'd been experiencing the last couple years were symptoms of menopause? It had never crossed my mind, because I'd always thought it was something that happened in your fifties or early sixties. My friends were still having babies, so it wasn't even on my radar. The more I read, though, the more things began to make sense, the more dots I was able to connect, in terms of both mental and physical health over the last couple years.

Looking back, I should have reached out sooner to tell the doctor that the herbal remedy wasn't working. Instead, I tried a different herbal remedy. I researched chronic pain and reread Dr. Sarno's book. I was trying to cope, trying to find my center—but we all were. It was hard to know what was causing what.

Every couple months, I tried to talk to the people in my life about it. Because none of my friends are experiencing menopause, they said, "Ooh, that sucks. I think my mom used like a cream or something?" They cared, but it was theoretical. Most people recommended cannabis or antidepressants.

We went away for a few days to a little ski town in Pennsylvania—Aaron's parents came for a few days, and then mine. And being away made it strikingly clear that I wasn't okay, not even a little. I was struggling and had been for a while, and it wasn't just about ambient stress or being tired. My mental and physical health were both significantly compromised and I was flailing. The first night my parents were there, we stayed up after the boys and Aaron went to bed, and I could see myself reflected in their eyes and I could see their concern too.

I went to the doctor again. I showed up with a list that felt like it was growing longer by the day: Insomnia and anxiety. I was gaining weight and craving super-weird foods. I was consumed by rage and had hot flashes that felt more like demon possession.

I have such acute memories of ripping off my clothes in my closet—it is categorically not a walk-in closet, but the kids were in our bedroom trying to talk with me about something, so I was in the tiny closet, clawing at my sweatshirt, gasping for air, breathless with rage. Sometimes it would happen in the kitchen—a narrow space with a window at the end—and I would press myself all the way to the window, trying to hide, trying to get some space, trying to regulate my breathing and my rage.

I remember a friend having a hot flash once when we were shopping together. She smiled and was a little embarrassed but was good-natured about the sweat beading on her forehead and temples—"Hot flash," she said with a shrug. That's what I thought it would be like, but for me it feels so much more like a rage episode, like a panic attack, like an adrenaline surge that comes when you almost crash a car. It feels like glass breaking and putting your head in an oven and being stuck in a crowd when you most want to hide. It scared me every time—the lack of predictability and the intensity of it.

My doctor said she'd start me on the hormone treatment as soon as I had a clean mammogram. I scheduled the mammogram, and after the mammogram, I was told to schedule an ultrasound imaging. The doctor who read those images scheduled a biopsy. Every appointment was at a different hospital or lab in the city, every one a place I'd never been. Every appointment was preceded by calls to the doctor for referrals to the lab and calls to the insurance company for approval of the recommended procedure.

I had stacks and stacks of forms and numbers and addresses that I kept adding to the pink folder. I had portals and instructions and confirmation calls, but no one talked to me about what anything meant. Technical terms, measurements. No lotion or perfume before a mammogram. No pain medication that could thin the blood before a biopsy. No one in the waiting room with me because of the pandemic.

I went to Union Square and Midtown and Lenox Hill and Columbus Circle. Sometimes I walked and sometimes I took an Uber—both the driver and I masked, a clear sheet of plexiglass separating us, windows open to the cold air, clutching my bright pink folder. After one of the mammograms, I walked home almost seventy blocks, most of it in the rain. I stopped at a fancy Upper East Side Italian restaurant that had a little outdoor shed and ordered a dirty martini, a Caesar salad, and an incredibly crisp chicken Milanese.

At the biopsy, the doctor told me that after she collected the samples she needed—five in all, after two numbing shots—she would insert a metal clip with the last needle, so that if "it" needed to come out (whatever "it" was), the next surgeon would know where it was. A scavenger hunt, sort of, and a clue. She assured me it wouldn't go off in a metal detector or at the airport or anything. She laughed, but I didn't know what was funny. I didn't know what was happening to me.

After the biopsy I walked by a Cuban restaurant and, full of adrenaline and relief, bought a huge amount of takeout—empanadas and shrimp in a garlicky green sauce and ropa vieja and plantains. I dragged that big bag home to the boys and then crawled in bed, the adrenaline suddenly gone. It was Tuesday. Someone somewhere told me to expect results by Friday, but it actually took a full week longer than that. I called every day, all different offices. By that next Friday I was vibrating with fear and anxiety. It was the Friday before Christmas.

By late morning, I couldn't focus my mind on anything else. I couldn't write. I couldn't shop for Christmas presents. I was just wandering, wearing a track in the apartment floor, staring out the window. I finally stopped pretending I was going to get anything done and instead made soup—onions, garlic, carrots. Tomatoes, peppers, white beans, spinach. Fennel, oregano, red pepper flakes. The chopping and the heat and the smells and sounds occupied me at least a little bit.

When the call finally came, it was about ten seconds long with a person I had never spoken to before. In a heavy accent she told me nothing was wrong. That's it—nothing was wrong. I asked if I could speak with the doctor or if I could come in for an appointment. "Why would you do that?" she asked. "Nothing is wrong." And then she hung up, and instead of relief or joy or laughter, I was flooded with rage.

Talk to me! I wanted to scream. *Explain it to me. Show it to me. Why was a biopsy even needed? What was it, and what is it, and why did I go through all this and why won't anyone talk to me about it?* Aaron was so relieved. My parents were so relieved. I wasn't there yet. Part of me was, but another part of me was still knotted up by the waiting and the fear.

The next night, we gathered for a friend's birthday—a small group, the same people with whom we'd been quarantining for months. A couple of us stayed for hours after everyone else left, our conversation turning from serious to funny to old stories to screaming with laughter. We had the windows wide open to the cold night sky, and for a couple hours I felt young and happy and carefree.

When I came back to our apartment super late, I realized

that the raisin bread we'd begun earlier that day had finished its third rise, so I preheated the oven and puttered around the apartment. I was practically asleep on the couch by the time the bread baked, and as I pulled the loaves out of the oven, I felt how deeply tired I was, not just because it was so late but because I had been holding my breath for nearly a month and could finally exhale.

Two weeks later, I got a letter in the mail. One page. It detailed the surgeon's actions and findings. A solid nodule, 1.3 centimeters in diameter, at the right three o'clock location. An 18-gauge spring-loaded needle. Five samples retrieved. The nodule determined to be a fibroid. Benign, and removal not necessary. The surgeon's first name, I noted, was Zeva, and I thought that was a beautiful name. She had been kind and efficient—a mother of twins, she'd told me.

I tucked that piece of paper into my bright pink folder.

thirty

Cold Moon

Near the end of December, near the winter solstice, there was a Cold Moon—a full December moon, shining like a spotlight. It was the darkest moment yet for me, in a season of dark moments. My mind kept coming back to the idea that I couldn't keep going, that I absolutely couldn't keep moving forward into the future. I wanted to stop, in every way. The phrase "mental breakdown" surfaced in my mind and stayed there a while.

I felt newly connected to my own feelings of rage. The mental health aspects of menopause became more and more intense right as the pandemic made our lives smaller and smaller, more and more cramped, and my rage felt sharpened to a point. I felt nearly out of control, as dark and dangerous as I'd ever felt in my life. I wanted to scream. I wanted to break dishes. I wanted to kick things. I wanted out of the apartment, but going outside the apartment meant being out in the cold and in the dark by about 4:00 p.m. I felt stuck to the point of caged, and it felt like my rage was squeezing us all, like a huge balloon inflating and flattening us against the walls of the already small space. I tried to step outside myself and remind myself that this was something happening to me, like a virus, like a wave. I tried to breathe through it, like a contraction.

I was at my wits' end, and I was scared and out of options, and so in desperation that I decided to try to befriend the rage. Maybe she could teach me something. Maybe she was trying to tell me something. Maybe this wasn't simply a surge of hormones but a guide of some kind, a weapon I could use to protect myself, a tool I could use to build a new self.

I'm learning to use the anger, to listen to it instead of holding myself separate from it, pretending it's a garment I can put on and take off. It's a part of me. These are my tears. This is my grief. This is my rage. I'm learning to own it and make space for it and tend to it instead of holding it at arm's length.

The insomnia is crazymaking, both because of the darkness of my thoughts and feelings in the night when I can't sleep and because of the toll that perpetual sleeplessness takes on my days. I'm caught in a cycle of simultaneously longing for bedtime and dreading bedtime, and also I've succumbed to every wacky sleep remedy there is—at bedtime these days, I chew melatonin gummies, drink sour magnesium powder in cold water, swallow herbal remedies, stick calming patches on my wrists. Nothing helps, or at least nothing helps enough.

I read whole novels in the night or go on weird internet deep dives or force myself not to reach for my phone and instead catalog all the worst things about myself or all the things I should have done but didn't. I wake up exhausted by my own mind, full of shame and contempt for myself, aching for relief or rest right when I should be starting the day.

That dark December night, I put myself to bed around 9:00 p.m., not because I was tired, especially, but because I needed to not be around any other people. I'd already snapped at the kids, apologized, snuggled, but that hot-flash rage was hovering like a ghost and I felt like I couldn't shake it all the way off, and for the health and safety of everyone in the apartment, I needed to be in bed.

I woke up the next morning with a sense of power—not hope, exactly, but a fizzing undercurrent of strength. Maybe menopause is sharpening the pain to a point, pushing me to deal with my anger more deeply and directly than I would have otherwise. It's peeling back the facades, stripping the defenses, leaving me with only my rage, which is the point, which is the next step. Maybe it's my superpower, my portal to my next self.

Yesterday's snow squall seems to me just exactly the right image to capture the whole of this season—sudden darkness, heavy wind, a wild, magical swirl of sideways snow that disrupted the whole city just for a little while.

The darkness, wind, and snow hit neighborhood by neighborhood, and we texted from Chelsea south to the West Village, further still to Tribeca—did it hit there yet? Now? Now?

Traffic was a tangle of chaos and plans were hastily canceled and rearranged. Our phones lit up and buzzed with alerts about something that was already very obvious, swirling all around us.

It was equal parts beautiful and disruptive—not the afternoon any of us expected, but an entirely different thing, entirely out of our control. It lifted us out of whatever we'd had planned and plopped us down into a snow globe, lovely and strange.

And that's just how this season feels to me. Not what I planned. Not what I expected. Darker, but also beautiful in a quiet, sort of strange way.

part four

Bloom

thirty-one

Magic Desk

After the New Year, I immersed myself in writing. I sat at my desk for hours on end and stared out at the city. I typed and cried and read and stared out at the city some more, until I remembered who I was, until life made sense again, until I could grasp just one corner edge of hope. That desk and those windows saved me.

For so many years what saved me was community, connection, action. I'm an ultimate verbal processor, so talking has always helped. Being with people healed me. Talking things through and getting advice and wisdom, asking for help—those are the things that used to help so much. But all of a sudden, the only place where anything made sense was at my desk. I sat and stared and wrote and cried, and little by little I remembered who I wanted to be again. I wrote when I was afraid and when I was sad and when I was filled with rage. I cried until I gagged and drank one thousand cups of lukewarm tea, and I just typed and typed and typed, pouring it all out until the energy inside me subsided a little bit, until I could breathe again. I wasn't writing anything amazing, by any means, but I was doing what I've always done—writing my way through the pain.

It wasn't about sharing the writing or connecting through it. It was about making sense of my life through words. It was about giving all the words a place to be outside my body, giving the pain and the fear and the suffering a place to be outside my body. It became the safest place in the world to me, my home base. When I had to do something hard—a phone call I knew would be difficult, a section of writing that felt tender—I came back to my desk. I could be powerful at the desk. I could say hard things at the desk. I could both protect myself and push myself at the desk. It became the place where this new self I was building, cell by cell, could start to learn the world and learn her own voice in it.

Of course there were other things—therapy, certainly. Walking. Talking with friends. But mostly, that desk and that chair and those windows were the cocoon I needed, a quiet place to start hearing my own voice again.

Sometimes when you're practicing yoga, the long-term practice, over time, starts to yield something. You feel, mostly, like you're just putting in your time, but little by little, you're surprised by the benefits, both in your yoga practice and in the rest of your life—it's working! It's subtle, and you don't always love the hour you spend doing it, but you can see the benefits and so you keep going.

But sometimes an entirely other thing happens—much more rarely in my experience. The actual time you spend on the mat transforms you as it's happening. You weep, maybe, or you feel alive in your body in an entirely new way. Things are changing in real time, in your body, in your spirit. Grief is being exorcised, released. Your breath is warm and powerful, sweeping through the rooms of your chest like wind, fresh and powerful.

I've had a similar experience with prayer and singing—mostly, I think of these practices as soul building in the long term, nutritious and healthy ways of living that will bolster me on hard days, investments in the future. But every once in a while, the act of praying feels connective and transformative in real time, or the act of singing a hymn or a worship song draws something emotional and powerful up and out of me like a long-buried thread.

And that's how writing has been for me recently—the most unconscious, out-of-control, deeply emotional experience I've yet had. My writing has swerved more closely to therapeutic or spiritual work than it ever has in my life.

One of the reasons I became a writer was that I liked what it brought about in my life. Writing helps me, heals me, provides a place for all my thoughts and feelings and words, a place for all the wild birds in my head and my heart to fly around outside of me instead of inside of me, because that's a hard way to live— with wild birds circling around your insides.

But like yoga and prayer, I've mostly experienced the healing part in the long term, in a sort of boring but worthwhile way. I write and write, and over time, I start to make sense of things. I start to see connections I didn't see before. I learn about myself and about the world.

But this time around has felt different. It has felt, in some moments, like a sort of otherworldly, deeply physical and emotional moving through, like this isn't just about my brain sorting letters into words and words into sentences. And it isn't just about the end result—having found meaning in some way, having arrived at a new understanding or perspective. It's more like the act of writing, the fingers on the keys, has been a healing act in real time.

I call it my magic desk, as completely silly as that is. One of the best things about my magic desk is that I can see Mac dance his way back to our building. Today he went to the front desk to pick up packages, and even with his arms full of boxes, he danced back, wiggling his hips and kicking, moonwalking and spinning.

We joke that I should be the captain of some sort of neighborhood watch program, for all the time I spend at this desk looking out over the courtyard. I know every branch and every brick. I know where each neighbor gets their groceries and when their dogs get taken out. I see every coming and going, and after all these months I'm attuned to the rhythm of it—people leaving for work and returning, people going back and forth to the library or the patio, morning prayer and evening prayer. Through it all, I'm still here, still watching the light in the trees, still writing my way to a new self, here at my little magic desk.

thirty-two

Energy in the Air

Yesterday, I felt exhaustion and hope, twinned. We're not through the darkness yet, but we came through something this week, the end of something. There will be hard things ahead, but not these same things.

I read on and off all day, stretched out like a cat, finding the light. I made a big weekend breakfast and prepped vegetables and cleaned the kitchen. When a couple of neighbor dads and boys came over to watch a movie with Aaron and our boys, I greeted them and chatted for a little bit before slipping out and walking all over the city—down Ninth to Bleecker to the West Village, all the way down to Carmine, back along Hudson and then along Tenth, all the way up to Twenty-Seventh. I must have stopped at ten places looking for a table without a two-hour wait, and even the terrible ones had lines out the door.

There were people everywhere, and you could feel the energy in the air—different, lively, pent up, distinctly young, a little frantic. Pastels, loud music, big groups of people weaving along the sidewalks, yelling and laughing. It felt like a totally different city, a totally different season.

When I finally found an available table, I sat alone, happily. I drank a dirty martini with a blue cheese olive and ordered a pizza with spicy salami and ricotta and I felt calm. A little hopeful. A little free.

We're still firmly in winter, but I see spring—in all the ways—holding out her hand to me. I'm not there yet, but I see it. I'm inching. I'm letting this city and this springtime thaw my inner winter, wake me up, pull me into life and light a little bit. But it's been a long winter, and so much has been buried in ice for so long.

The next day, I woke up to my new morning routine. I begin by feeling the unfeelable feelings and thinking the unthinkable thoughts.

Second, I forgive. I forgive the night. I forgive the people who have hurt me. I forgive the world for not being what I wanted. I forgive myself for all the ways I feel like I'm failing.

Then I make space for desire: What do I want? I want healing. I want to move through the pain and leave it behind. I want lightness and freedom of spirit. Andrew, my beloved therapist, encouraged me to set aside a time every day to feel the sadness. I knew the power of the magic desk, but I forgot for a couple days, so I went back and wrote out the questions:

What's happening inside me? What's happening around me? What might I need to learn or unlearn or face right now? Am I offering deep kindness and forgiveness toward myself, deep kindness and forgiveness for others? Am I tending lovingly to myself and others? What do I need to walk away from or walk toward? What requires my participation or voice?

I kept writing, kept asking questions, kept making space for grief and forgiveness and pain and desire. I kept walking, willing spring to come, around me and inside me.

And then there was a moment when I was walking up the stairs to our apartment alone, hand on the wobbly banister, mind churning. After so much grief, so much wrestling, so much pleading—*I don't want this to be my life!*—I felt that click of acceptance. Something inside me said, clear as an audible word, *I can live inside this life. I can make myself a home in this story. People make it through all kinds of things, and I can make it through this. I can, and I am.*

thirty-three

On Resurrection

In the spring, as buds began to bloom and days got longer, when the Javits Center was transformed into a massive vaccination center, the city began to wake up, and we did too—little by little, emerging from such a long and desolate freeze. We went to the Museum of Natural History, and to Rockaway Beach for the first time. We packed up our snow boots and dug out the picnic blanket.

On Easter Sunday, several families gathered on the patio—mimosas, pimento cheese, deviled eggs, leg of lamb. We stayed around the tables until the sun set behind the buildings, cool and dark all of a sudden. But before that, a strange and wonderful afternoon—unfamiliar after all these months of isolation, and all the sweeter for it. The kids ran back and forth, searching for eggs, trading candy, sneaking cupcakes. And the grown-ups shuffled around, scraping back chairs from the table to start new conversations, catching up with other families and friends. It was something we'd ached for for so many months and we reveled in it. Resurrection, indeed. New life, indeed.

Easter is sort of a gruesome holiday—you don't get to the eggs or the pastels or the new life without confronting a violent death and a silent and desolate Saturday. It's a hard-won celebration, and never more so than this year. We all remarked that we couldn't really remember Easter last year because it was a day just like any other in those early quarantine days—isolated in our homes, weighted with uncertainty and fear.

This year, then, felt doubly effervescent, teeming with life and possibility. Easter is when life triumphs over death, but still there is grief, still there is loss, still there is the darkness of Holy Week, the silence of Saturday. I'm grateful for every shred of new life on Easter, and also I'm bruised a little—we all are—by the intensity of the losses of this last year. We needed Easter this year more than ever, and also we see it with a little more clarity this year—life triumphs over death, indeed, but not always in real time. Life triumphs over death, indeed, but not in many of the ways we've been longing for.

One of the many, many gifts of living on an Episcopal seminary campus is the ongoing awareness of the church calendar. It's like we're living inside a calendar with reminders everywhere we look, bells throughout the day to mark morning and evening prayers.

And one of my favorite physical reminders happens during Holy Week. The Chapel of the Good Shepherd—the center point of the seminary both architecturally and spiritually—has huge, heavy, carved metal doors, and they're always open—all night long, all throughout the year, except for one time. On Good Friday, we gather for an evening service, and the service ends with the blowing out of the candles, leaving us in darkness and silence. We walk out in silence, and we stand in silence on the lawn outside the chapel, and we watch as those ornate doors are closed with a heavy clank.

The doors stay closed all day on Saturday, and it's jarring, a little bit, every time you walk by to pick up mail or do laundry. You don't realize how used to those open doors you've become until they're closed, and your eye catches them every time, that strong intuitive sense that something's not as it should be. Because it isn't. I love the stark imagery of it. I love the reminder of it, all day long on Holy Saturday.

And then early on Sunday morning, a priest unlocks those doors before anyone is out and about, and there's that sense that all is right, that all is as it should be, the doors open, peace and hope restored once again. An open door, an empty tomb, life after death.

thirty-four
On Painting Badly

My therapist recommended that I start painting—something creative that wasn't word-based, something expressive that wasn't so literal. And so the boys and I went to Blick Art Materials one unseasonably warm afternoon. I told them they could each pick one thing—pastels or acrylics or whatever—and the right paper or canvas to use with it. We wandered all over, asked a million questions, weighed the pros and cons of all the options. It was inspiring just to be in that huge basement space, surrounded by canvases and colors and brushes. I've never been a painter or visual artist of any kind, but both boys love art, and I was desperate enough to try anything.

Later that evening, we put on some music and set up our paints all over the living room—Henry and I across from each other at the tiny dining table, Mac at the coffee table. I made some truly terrible first tries, but I kept going, dipping my brush into the water and then swirling it in the paints. We've pulled out the paints a handful of times since then, and though I can't say I'm going to frame anything I've painted, there is something calming about it—and truly unuseful.

That's important for me, I think. I like cooking because it's creative and it makes something. I liked making beaded bracelets and necklaces during the early pandemic days because I had something concrete to show for it. I had nothing to show for these painting nights except very, very bad watercolors, and that felt significant in and of itself. It was for its own sake, the doing of it, for what it did in my body and my breath and my brain, for the time I spent next to my kids, lost in color, slowing my breathing, rolling my shoulders down and back, down and back.

It's easy to want everything we do to be productive or valuable in an immediate way—like maybe I was going to discover some sort of profound but latent talent at forty-four years old and all of a sudden watercolor would be my life. That's grind culture, hustle culture, productivity culture, that voice that tells us we are what we make, what other people can see, what we can monetize. I cannot monetize my watercolors. I can barely look at them. My kids even know that I'm terrible—they say, *Oh, yeah, wow.* I'm like, "Don't *oh, yeah, wow* me." I've been doing the *oh, yeah, wow* noises for nearly fifteen years. I know what it means. And I agree with them. These are horrible. And that's the point. That there are spaces in my life that heal me and help me and don't build or provide or create anything beyond that. Healing me is enough. Helping me is enough.

It's back to embracing that beginner thing—if you have to be great at everything you do, you can't learn anything new, because the learning process is inherently about failing and trying again, figuring it out in messy and circuitous ways. It's hard and fumbling, and that's how any of us learn anything at all. Doing something badly is humbling and sometimes it's frustrating, and for those of us who are used to being experts, it's categorically worth every second.

thirty-five

A Movable Feast

Ten years ago, I was on a work trip to Dallas, and on my last morning there, I asked my old friend Sarah if she was free for breakfast and if she could drop me off at the airport afterward. She came to pick me up, and I wasn't really paying attention to where she was taking me—she has great taste and totally knows the city, so I was happy to be in her hands and knew we'd have a great meal no matter where she took me. I was staying at a hotel by the airport and assumed we'd head away from the airport, but instead we were heading right to it. At the last second, right before turning into the departures area, she pulled into the driveway of a small car wash.

"Okay, we're here," she announced. And she got out of the car and walked on the grass around the side of a small brick building. I followed her, and in this little grassy area behind a car wash about five hundred yards from the runway at DFW, there were a table and two chairs, along with a tablecloth, a bouquet of flowers, and two place settings. There were berries and croissants and eggs—and I was just absolutely confused and delighted. "Sarah! What is happening?"

She smiled and told me to sit down. "I know you've been busy, and I wanted to give you a little space and beauty and time. I wanted us to have a chance to really connect before you

147

leave. I looked for a place between your hotel and the airport, and I stopped in earlier this week and asked the car wash guy if I could use the lawn before they opened. I threw this stuff in the back of my car so we could share some time together."

I absolutely cried. It was so moving to hear someone say, *I wanted to make something special for you. I wanted to create a space for us.*

Hospitality is powerful. It can move us. It can heal us. It can remind us that we're loved, that we matter, that someone cares we're alive.

When I think about extraordinary hospitality moments and experiences, I don't think about fine dining or perfect meals or high-end artwork in fancy homes; I think about a card table outside a car wash, and how my friend Sarah communicated love, care, and thoughtfulness so powerfully to me in that moment.

Hospitality is holding space for another person to be seen and heard and loved. It's giving someone a place to be when they'd otherwise be alone. It's, as my friend Sibyl says, when someone leaves your home feeling better about themselves, not better about you.

For many of us in recent months, we've been forced to think about hospitality differently. Almost everyone I know experienced a disruption of gathering—at least the way it used to be. And almost everyone I know figured out a way to gather—even though it was weird.

My high school friends—whom I love but had never Zoomed with—started a Zoom happy hour tradition. An old friend and I set a date for a nightcap phone call. For Thanksgiving, we gathered outside for dessert with our neighbors—in New York in November in hats and jackets. At a French café in the West

Village on a snowy night, they handed out Mylar blankets, and when the wind blew in sideways to the outdoor dining area, and with it icy snowflakes, each table of guests screamed like we were doing the wave—"Agh! Agh! Agh!"—when the ice hit our faces. It was weird, but we still gathered.

I heard of friends meeting for takeout in parking lots with lawn chairs between their parked cars. My in-laws put a rug and chairs in their garage, so that with the door open, they could see family, even through the winter in the Midwest.

For a person who loves gathering and feeding people and every part of hospitality, I was determined to figure out a way to keep connecting, and for us that meant a picnic blanket and sheet pan. In New York, we couldn't gather indoors, but we could gather outside and so we did—over and over and over—with a picnic blanket and a sheet pan of snacks.

I have all manner of fancy cheeseboards—marble and slate and pretty ceramic. But here's the thing: when you're carrying food down three flights of stairs and then setting it on the ground, a sheet pan works a lot better than slate or marble.

Sometimes those happy hour cheeseboards were fancy—brie and lavender honey and prosciutto and rosé. And sometimes it was like Jonathan had half a box of crackers, Kate had apples and popcorn, and Kyndi had a few cans of sparkling water. I went through a prolonged queso phase, and one day Julia had leftover pizza dough that she baked into delicious garlicky breadsticks.

We watched beautiful spring weather arrive—breezy and bright, buds on branches glowing as the sun dropped lower and lower, illuminating each leaf and branch. Everything glowed green on the Close, our green space at the center of the seminary. One day, Kyndi brought grilled pimento cheese on baguettes and Jonathan brought cider from the craft beer shop on the corner. The next day, I brought red wine and pretzels with a couple different mustards. Other neighbors wandered over, some we knew well and some we didn't. The kids circled by from time to time for handfuls of crackers or clementine slices.

Sometimes we'd order pizza, and there was one night we stayed out there so long that we finished all the snacks and all the pizza but nobody wanted to leave, so I just kept running up and down the stairs with handfuls of things, and it was somewhere between a buffet and a yard sale.

It started a tradition that has now taken on a life of its own. I reach for my picnic blanket more often than I do my purse these days, and the picnic basket practically packs itself. It's that connection point, every day or every couple days—*how are we?* It used to be that the Close was the respite from the crush and craziness of the city. These days it's the respite from the isolation and crampedness of apartment living, distance learning, Zoom everything.

Let's all agree not to go back to that old way where the house has to be perfect and the food has to be perfect and the dishes have to be perfect. Get a sheet pan and a picnic blanket and have everyone bring a handful of things from their own kitchens.

Because it never was about the food. It never was about the dishes or the fancy kitchen tools or the complicated techniques. We just wanted to connect. This is how deeply the value of hospitality is planted inside us. Look how creative we've gotten.

Something miraculous happens when we gather. There's a connection, a healing, a nourishing that goes beyond the nutrients and calories and vitamins and minerals. There's a nourishing of spirit, and if we've learned anything at all through the pandemic, it's that we really need that connection, all of us. We need to see each other's faces and hear each other's voices. We need to laugh together and cry together and sit in silence together. We were made for connection, for sitting shoulder to shoulder, for carrying one another, walking together.

We've all experienced that phenomenon of getting used to people who are different than we are—at first, all you see are the differences and you sometimes trip over yourself trying to make sense of languages or accents or traditions that feel unfamiliar, but then over time, what was once foreign starts to feel very normal, like just another part of your world.

But the opposite is also true—and a season of prolonged isolation has not brought out the best in our culture. The political and religious and cultural differences became louder and more divisive. One antidote is hospitality, which requires bravery, intention, and a willingness to extend beyond ourselves in service of others. Being a Christian means devoting ourselves increasingly to the purposes of God on earth, to bringing the kingdom of heaven to earth in big and small ways.

A few weeks ago, I was invited to a party—a celebration of a friend's birthday. It was a gathering together of different worlds, and I knew I wouldn't know anyone except the birthday girl. I was feeling overwhelmed with going anywhere, and here I was, going all the way to a neighborhood I'd never been to, and I walked in the wrong door and couldn't figure out where I was and I felt frumpy—even though I had liked my dress at home, I immediately hated it when I walked in.

And then I had such interesting conversations with such interesting people—people who had lived very different lives than my own. I stayed about three hours longer than I thought I would—listening and laughing and getting to know these friends of friends I'd been hearing about for ages but had never met.

Because people are great. And we need each other and we have so much to learn from one another. And I had sort of forgotten that, because I hadn't been around very many for so long. Hospitality is the antidote to isolation, and we need it. I need it. Every neighborhood and town and city block needs it. And each one of us can be a part of it.

So keep gathering, keep it weird, embrace the movable feast, and practice brave, awkward, difficult hospitality as a way of fighting against isolation and othering, a way of healing what's been broken and loving our world and our own selves back to life.

thirty-six

Living Lightly Redux

This spring I'm releasing so many things, especially things that are tied to memories of a self I don't think I'll ever be again. That's what getting rid of these things is about—consenting to the reality that I'll never again fit into that dress, that I'll never be that person I see so clearly in my head. It doesn't mean I'll never feel beautiful again, but if I do, it won't be in that dress. There's something there for me, embracing age in a good way, a new self emerging in all sorts of ways, and with that, a willingness or ability to let go of those other selves, the ones I used to be, the ones I was still hanging on to.

This is the question: What do we keep? What do we let go because it makes us lighter, because it opens up space, because it keeps us right in the moment and location of where we are, not yearning for a world that doesn't exist anymore, a self that doesn't exist anymore? And what do we keep because it's part of the story of who we are, not just in this moment, but over years and decades, our essential selves?

I'm getting rid of dresses that felt right in the Midwestern summer but never feel right in the city. Sneakers that give me blisters every single time, no matter the Band-Aid/heel pad/moleskin regimen. Half a dozen cozy fleeces that are perfect for an UpNorth campfire but have never made it out of the closet here. Blouses I've always hated but kept because they worked well enough—life is hard enough without walking around with something on your body that makes you feel bad.

But even with all that sorting and selling and giving away, even with all the donate bags and hand-me-down bags and clearing away, this week my closet is telling me I'm still holding on to too much, to too many selves and stories that aren't being told anymore, that aren't exactly true anymore.

In almost all the ways—internal and external both—I've kept too much and let go of too little. It feels a little bit like shedding, a gradual process.

I like the idea of having a trunk or a section of a closet somewhere, someday, where I show my kids or grandkids the shoes I wore when . . . or the leather jacket I wore when . . . but I think what I'll do instead is tell them the story. I'll let the story live, let the memory be a part of me forever . . . and sell the shoes.

I'm letting go of lots of little-kid stuff I'd been holding on to—the action figures and Harry Potter wands, the puzzles without all the pieces, the Cubs jerseys that the boys have outgrown and the little suits that are too short. I'm letting go of the platters and bowls—how many platters did I think I needed? How many serving bowls, in an apartment that doesn't even fit a kitchen table?

This spring I'm letting go of the past I'd been holding, and the future too. This morning at school drop-off there was a woman with a perfectly white bob, and I loved it. Just a couple days ago, I felt the same pull. In a catalog, one of the women had silver hair and bright lipstick and I kind of wanted to be her. I was staring at it for a minute and one of my sons leaned over my shoulder and said, "Is that you, Mom?"

"I think so," I said. "I think it is."

thirty-seven

Rooftop

Last night, several of us sat up on the rooftop, drinking red wine and telling stories. A few around the table were in their forties, and a few in their twenties, and at first it was mostly jokes and good-natured outrage—*You were born the year I got my driver's license? I was in college when you were a toddler? You were in grade school for 9/11? That's the year I got married!*

As we talked, I was struck by another very stark difference: they had *plans*, those twentysomethings around the table. They had timelines and goals and plans—PhD by thirty, or sommelier by thirty-two. Marriage by thirty-five or living in Denver by next school year. And we didn't talk about it, but those of us on the other side of the table just nodded. Sounds good. Sounds like a plan. Sounds like the things we said, absolutely, when we were in our twenties—before most of the plans we made turned to dust in our hands.

In my late twenties, I was fired from a job I loved at a church where Aaron worked too, and all our friends—a church in a town we moved to only for that job, so once I didn't work there any longer, my life was very quiet and very painful.

In my early thirties, I had multiple miscarriages, one requiring extensive medical intervention and follow-up and then a long stretch of infertility. We sold a house in the middle of a recession, which I don't recommend, and moved back to our hometown, bruised and shaken.

The first couple years of my forties were like living in a blender—lots of bad and lots of good, but all of it together, loud and fast, one thing after another. It should tell you something that moving to Manhattan, of all places, was a respite—that's how intense the preceding seasons had been.

And so we looked at the young faces on the rooftop, or at least I did, and I recognized my younger self and admired their skin, and also I decided in that moment not to be a voice of doom and aging—*Oh sure, like you're in charge. Nice plans. Can't wait till life intervenes a thousand times and you look in the mirror and barely recognize your own face.* I just sat there, thinking about who I was all those years ago, what I believed about the world, what I wanted, what I'd planned.

I tried at one point to say that old reassuring thing— "thirties better than twenties, forties better than thirties"— maybe I wanted to believe it? In some ways it's true. But I also noticed a conspicuous silence from the women on either side of me.

"I don't know," one said, "my thirties were pretty great." The other said, "I mean, it's like the second I turned forty, things got really hard."

"You know what," I admitted, "you're right. I take it back. Twenties are better than teens. Thirties better than twenties. But so far, my forties are kind of a train wreck, and I'm sorry I tried to tell you differently. I *want* it to be different so very badly. But it's hard and chaotic and sad and stressful, and sometimes it's the right thing to just say that. It's hard right now, at least for me."

There is a privilege in getting to say, "I don't know"—it's not something you can always say in your first couple professional environments. It's not something you can say on a test and still pass. For women and persons of color especially, knowing is a necessity to enter or remain in environments dominated by white men.

But also, there's so much we don't know, all of us. And the world would be a healthier, more honest, safer place for all of us if curiosity were seen as a virtue, not a weakness. Those of us who have power of any kind have a responsibility to every younger person or every person who feels pressure to pretend they know more than they do.

We're responsible to help create a world that values questions more than answers, that celebrates learning and not just knowing, that sees failure as a part of the process of success.

I wanted to whisper across the table, "It's different than you think—time is different, plans start to look different, nearly every single thing looks different through my midforties eyes than what you're seeing through your fresh, bright, twenty-something eyes."

It's like they're on a scavenger hunt, ticking things off a list, building a life piece by piece, decision by decision: *City?* Check. *Job?* Check. *Significant other?* Check.

And we've built those lives and dismantled them, taken them apart piece by piece in a heavy and laborious way. We know what each decision cost, what it weighed. We know now, through the lens of time and heartbreak, which shiny moments ended up not so shiny in the rearview.

Another part of me doesn't want to tell them anything. They'll find out soon enough, like we all do, and a know-it-all Debbie Downer with crow's feet isn't going to tell them anything before they learn it on their own. I remember all the people I didn't listen to, people who were older than me, people who tried to tell me about loss and uncertainty and the pain of watching your precious plans turn to dust in your hands. "Sounds terrible," I murmured, hoping to distance myself from whatever bad juju they might be spreading on me. Because I had a plan. Didn't we all?

I don't have their beauty or their skin or their ease, but what I coveted, up there on the rooftop, was their years—not in terms of skin or fine lines, but in terms of actual math. They're at the beginning of so many things, and I'm in the rough and ugly middle, plenty of regrets and scars and mistakes, months and years I can never get back. But also, everything led us here. Could it have been any other way?

These days, I feel like my plans exist in two manifestations: extreme close-up and very far-off lists. Like today I need to go to the dry cleaner, and someday I want enough bookshelves for all my books, but everything between those things is pretty fuzzy. Also, for the record, I probably won't make it to the dry cleaner today. This is midlife.

Aaron and I were talking on the way home. "Remember," he said, "when we thought forty was super old, and that when you were forty, you'd know absolutely everything? You'd be done feeling uncertain and all the big pieces would be figured out. Remember?" And then we laughed loudly together for a long time like it was a hilarious joke.

thirty-eight

Never Too Late

Years ago, a man heard about two young refugees in his small town who needed temporary housing. These teenage brothers had come to this small town through a local relief agency from worlds away—literally the other side of the globe. They spoke very little English, were separated from their families, and didn't know anyone but each other. They needed a place to live. They needed computer skills and driver's licenses and language classes. They needed help grocery shopping and enrolling in classes.

A man named Bob volunteered—somewhat begrudgingly. His politics didn't align, necessarily, with the refugee cause. He was entirely unfamiliar with the part of the world these young people came from, and he was a little apprehensive about their religious practices. But he was a dependable volunteer and a person committed to practicing generosity, and so he prepared his guest room for a temporary stay for these boys.

A temporary stay extended, and extended, and extended. He taught them to use computers and tracked down used computers for them. He taught them to drive, with orange traffic cones in his driveway to simulate parking spots. He took them to get driver's licenses and to their language classes. He helped them buy used cars. He learned about their country and their traditions and their religion. He asked them to teach him about the foods they missed, because he wanted to learn to fix those meals for them.

He immersed himself in immigration law and process, and woe to the individual who picked up the phone when he was calling to check on the status of a form or visa. He was their advocate, their mentor, their friend.

He helped them get jobs, and when they started dating, they brought their girlfriends to dinner to meet Bob. When one of their girlfriends needed to go back to her country of origin for visa reasons, it was Bob who accompanied her and her young son. He became a father figure, and they became like sons and daughters. He talked about them with so much pride, and he became loyal to and enamored with their home countries, their traditions, their favorite foods.

He changed their lives. And they absolutely changed his.

Bob was my grandpa, Robert Lawrence Barry, and he died last month just shy of his ninety-first birthday. In the weeks before his passing, we all shared stories about this extraordinary community that began with what was supposed to be a weekend stay. These two young men, and eventually their wives and their children—all these lives—have been so powerfully shaped by the generosity and commitment of one man, and he'd be quick to say that they taught him more and gave him more than he ever gave them.

Here's an important aspect of this story: my grandpa met these young men when he was eighty-five years old. This incredible story, these very rich and meaningful and transformative relationships—this all happened in five years.

My grandpa had been recently widowed, and he was looking for something to occupy his time. That's how it started.

He just wanted to help a little, to use what he had, which was time and space.

He was a person of uncommon and truly fierce vitality. I'll be honest with you, I'm forty-four, and there are times when I think, *Well, I'm probably done with cardio—that's a young woman's game.* Or I'm willing to admit that I don't understand the first thing about, say, cryptocurrency or TikTok, and I'm okay with that. And then I think of my grandpa. For more than ninety years he was still learning, still discovering, still changing, and still opening his heart. His vitality and curiosity make me stand up, stretch, ask questions, learn. At a time in life when most people are winding down and settling into routines, Grandpa did the opposite.

If you think you're too old to make a difference, you're not. If you think you don't have enough time left to build something really beautiful, you're wrong. If you think your legacy-leaving window has closed, it hasn't.

It's not too late for you. And it's not too late for me. My grandpa was an unusual, opinionated, very tough man, and he began a life-altering journey right at the time when many people's lives are nearly over.

There's still time. You can still grow into something beautiful. You can still leave something lasting and nourishing. It's never, ever too late to grow.

thirty-nine

Bloom

Outside the door to our apartment building, there's a huge, gorgeous tulip magnolia. On Sunday, the buds were still tightly wrapped around themselves, but on Tuesday night, we stopped our conversation to marvel at this tree—lush blooms arching wide and open like ballerinas doing backbends, a perfect blowsy magenta with a sweeter, softer pink at the stems.

Spring is a reminder, of course, of the ephemeral reality of everything. These blooms will be gone by the weekend, never to be seen again till next year. Time marches on. Nature marches on.

The shift of seasons invites familiar rhythms—the kids running around the courtyard in big packs from one end to the other, little gangs going from the lounge to the playground, stopping just long enough to see what kind of snacks we're having, grabbing crackers and pickles every time they run by.

With each passing month during this spring, I felt myself coming back to life in fits and starts. I don't know that I've ever felt so deeply connected to the turning of springtime as I did this time—partially, probably, because I was so desperate for it, and partially because I had a front-row seat to it every day, watching every bud and branch, every greening by degree.

Aaron was finishing up his last classes and projects to

complete his master's degree. Henry was finishing eighth grade, and we were working on high school applications. Mac became a very valued customer at the French bakery on the corner, and the last week in April, his elementary school went back in-person full-time—he was delighted and didn't want to be walked to school anymore. Did I ever imagine I'd have a nine-year-old who'd walk himself to school in Manhattan? Add that to the list of things I never could have seen coming, but that delights me nonetheless.

As I'm on this side of the winter, I wonder, though, if that lowest low point back in December was a dark gift for me—it forced me to get more help, more support, to reach out to my doctor and therapist, to read and learn and practice a more self-compassionate way of living. Maybe it's the care I engaged in after that day that enabled me to get through the next few months without a similar drop into darkness, even while the events of my life were impossibly difficult, painful, and chaotic in ways I never could have imagined.

I know how to get through days when you feel like your actual bones might be breaking under the weight of your grief. I know how to get through days when you count the hours till bedtime before you even get out of bed in the morning. I know how to get through.

I know to ask for help, drink water, double down on therapy and sleep. I know to get outside and be on the lookout for beauty, especially in nature, and to read poetry and cookbooks for comfort. I know that making soup keeps your hands busy and passes the time when you're waiting for biopsy results.

I know that a lot of things come around eventually, that relationships get repaired, that the hot sizzle of pain fades to an ache over time, that fresh air helps everything and sugar makes everything worse, at least for me. I know I'm not the only one who has been through hard things—far from it.

Flowers are still blooming, show-offy and bright. The world is still good, still beautiful, still dazzling and interesting and worth tasting and finding and savoring. God is still good, still faithful, still kind. There's a lot I don't know, but there's enough that I do.

forty

How to Stay

For Emily

There's a handful of reasons people call me—for a book recommendation or for advice on where to eat in a particular city. Painting with a wide brush, I'm going to recommend John O'Donohue's *To Bless the Space Between Us*, Anne Lamott's *Traveling Mercies*, and Louise Penny's Inspector Gamache series to almost every living human. Also, Quartino in Chicago, The Southerner in Saugatuck, Canlis in Seattle, and Roberta's in Brooklyn.

Another reason people call? Because they're having a miscarriage or someone they know is having one. I hate these calls, because I hate what they're experiencing, but I also know that it helps to talk to someone who knows.

Some go like this: The bleeding just started. What do I do? Some like this: I'm in the car, just left the ultrasound, no heartbeat. I've received messages and phone calls like this from all over the world, from old friends and near strangers alike, because I'm the only one they know who has talked about this part of life. It's by no means because I'm the only person in their life who has experienced it. Statistically, one in four pregnancies ends in miscarriage. But we don't talk about it well or openly, so on top of the grief is the loneliness that adds so much weight to an already nearly crushing reality.

I miscarried the first time when Henry was eighteen months old. I was eleven weeks, and it was a molar pregnancy, which is rare and complicated, and one of the hardest parts of it is the months you have to wait to try again and the bazillion blood tests along the way. The second miscarriage was difficult in other ways—because it was the second, because it came after several years of infertility and a hard move, because I found out there was a problem just before speaking the eulogy at my grandmother's funeral, and because it was twins, and I lost one and then the other, days apart. I am a reluctant expert on this topic, and I'm honored to pick up the phone call when needed.

And then the last category: I get a call when someone has stopped believing something about God and essentially wants to know if that thing they're leaving behind means they should just leave it all behind. I'm the one you call when the faith you've clung to for years or even decades is no longer viable, for whatever reason . . . because a church or pastor failed you, because you've been kicked out in formal or far subtler ways, because you have questions that aren't welcome, because prayer feels like speaking into a void all of a sudden, because whatever your religious or spiritual practice has been, it isn't anymore and you're scared. Scared sometimes or lonely or angry or weary or all of the above.

I love these calls, because on the other end of the phone is someone who is afraid and sad and wants to know that there is life on the other side of this confusion, this crisis—and I know there is. I love getting to say that over and over and over to people I love. There are a million ways to be a Christian. There are a million ways to live your faith. It can be so difficult sometimes to find fellow travelers who speak your same language of faith, but it's worth it to hunt for them.

This is a conversation people bring to me like a secret, in a whisper, looking around to make sure no one hears. It always feels like a confession, like I'm a priest, and the person who's telling me waits just a little bit, waiting for me to freak out about what they've just told me. I hold their gaze, hold the weight of what they've just told me, hold steady.

I nod slowly. *Yes, yes, I hear you. I'll hold this with you. You're going to be okay. You're not the only one. There is a way through.*

I've always said that the reason I love officiating weddings is because I get to bear witness to the actual creation of an entirely new family, like being a midwife but without all the blood and screaming. And this is the same process—midwifery of the spiritual sort, ushering in a new way of living and being. As with childbirth, there are absolutely moments when you feel like you're dying, and there are moments when you think you will or that your faith is dead, beyond resuscitation.

You will not die, and your faith won't either. But it will change.

There have been more than enough reasons for me to give up on Jesus, give up on the church, walk away from hope and faith. Haven't most of us been given enough reasons?

But I can't shake it. More accurately, I can't find the parts of myself that would remain if I tried to cleave away the spiritual parts. I think about a surgeon using a scalpel to separate cancerous cells from healthy ones or cut the scar tissue from healthy tissue. I feel like if you opened my chest and sliced open my heart, it would be impossible to discern which are spiritual cells and which are just the plain old ones. The yeast has been worked through the dough, and nothing now can separate the two. This is God's work, not mine. This is a gift, not an accomplishment.

My friend Hannah and I walked along the Hudson River one fall morning, and she said, "The church is a mess—in its own right, politically, in terms of gender and race—and it's getting so much wrong. How do you stay?"

"I see all that," I told her. Of course I do. But there's a stubborn part of me that is absolutely unwilling to starve my own heart because some other people have gotten it wrong. My faith is one of the most nourishing, healing, restorative parts of my life, and I'm unwilling to go without it as a protest. I see the church's failings. I've seen many of them up close, much closer than I'd like. But show me something that hasn't been corrupted by human hands. And my hands are as fallible as any. I still believe that the way of Jesus, even poorly done, is a better way than any other.

I sat with an old friend in the courtyard. She was in the city for a few days, and we had a little picnic surrounded by the redbrick buildings. She told me about the split second when she realized with absolute clarity that the institutions she had trusted all her life had failed her. She used the word *unanchored*—nearly everyone does in this process.

I nodded, listening. "I know," I said. I know. Let me tell you what happens. You realize that the institutions and structures and systems you've been trusting all your life aren't actually going to save you or keep you safe—that they never were going to, that they never could. And you start to fall, and it's terrifying. It's awful and dark and you don't know where the bottom is or who's going to catch you and then one day you realize you are there, on the bottom. And under it all—under all the institutions and plans and systems, under all your fear and longing and tears, under absolutely everything—is love.

Picture yourself on the ocean floor after all that falling,

having left behind your successes and triumphs, your ego and shiny self, your deal-making and false assurances. At the bottom of it all, there is love.

"What you do," I told my friend as we sat in the grass, "is you stay there on the bottom of the ocean for a while. And little by little, you begin to build a little shelter for yourself, built on a foundation of love. You build with a prayer and then maybe a poem. You build a window and a door and a roof out of love and honesty and compassion. You ask the wisest people you know, and the kindest.

"You reread the words of Jesus and the Psalms. You trust that love will hold it all together, and over time you realize that this tiny shelter you've built around yourself suits you much better than those grand institutions ever did, because this one was built out of pain and loss and disillusionment, forged by confession, prayer, longing. Once you build this shelter, you bring it everywhere you go."

This is the process of a lifelong faith. Born again. Again. Again. You won't have to unravel and rebuild in such a comprehensive way every time—it seems to me that most people have several faith disruptions over a lifetime. But there are smaller quakes along the way too, and what a gift we would give ourselves if we could normalize this process. The Christian tradition is inherently in motion—a people walking through the wilderness, a Savior walking the road to Calvary, an ongoing journey—life, death, rebirth.

When I was in high school, my mom—raised as a conservative Baptist and at that point the wife of the founding pastor of a very large, very public church—found herself in a crisis of faith, a deep and all-encompassing spiritual darkness. Attending church felt violating. Pretending felt impossible.

Spiritual business as usual was no longer an option. My dad told the elders about what my mom was experiencing. He told them she needed space and time and freedom to figure out this part of her life, without thousands of people watching. For most of my high school years, she didn't attend services. She read and prayed and sought out mentors. She learned about Celtic mystic traditions and contemplative practices, and for a long time, the only sections of the Bible she read and reread were the words of Jesus.

She emerged from that time with a deep faith forged through experience. She began traveling to the poorest and most war-torn places on earth—not the most usual course for a Midwestern pastor's wife, but the next natural step for a deep-feeling social work major who came to understand her faith as a marriage of action and contemplation, two necessary sides of the coin.

Watching her marked me. It made me unafraid of the journey of faith—to expect it, even. She showed me during those years that faith is something you tend to, something you nurture, something you dismantle and rebuild, something you wrestle with because it matters that much to you. And watching our church's elders marked me too. It would have been easier, maybe, for them to insist on appearances, on business as usual. But they didn't. I'm sure they had to answer hard questions about it from time to time, and I'm so grateful they were willing to care for our family in that way—it was the harder choice, but the better one.

We have regular conversations these days with our kids about the process of faith, not just the fact of it. We tell them it's something that changes over time, something we have to tend to. We talk with them in age-appropriate ways about how doubt is a part of faith, about how questions are normal, about how our faith stretches and expands inside our hearts over time, about how it's not the same in every season.

There are a million reasons not to stay. I could list several hundred thousand, at least. Many of our churches are sick, infected by racism and patriarchy. Many use shame and fear as ways to control. Many use manipulation and charm. There are so many reasons to walk away.

But nothing gets healed or restored or brought back to life unless those of us who still believe in hope, in honesty, in confession and prayer and the sacred reality of the church gathered keep gathering, keep working, keep praying, keep making changes. And so I stay.

I hold on to the fact that God is. And he is love, which is the center of everything. We've gotten approximately one billion things wrong along the way, it seems, as we've built governments and systems and institutions and, certainly, religions. We've built them in our image, with the structures and shapes that make sense to us—power, control, hierarchy. Bigger is better. Faster is better. Pretty and thin matter more than smart and kind, because those first things are the ones you can observe through a screen—and who has time anymore for boring and unsexy things like thinking and morality? I say that not to shame us but to encourage us to change course. We don't have to live like this. We can dismantle and rebuild. And we must.

I'm choosing faith that loves quiet, humility, mystery. I'm choosing a tradition that begins with creativity, dust, words, love. That's who we are, who we've always been—created on purpose, shaped by a word, loved beyond measure.

part five

Still Yes

forty-one

Recovering

It's a hot, sunny morning and the boys are at Rockaway Beach. They dug out their swimsuits for the first time in ages while I packed up chips and granola bars and clementines, water bottles and towels and sunblock.

Yesterday we spent the afternoon with friends on the patio. We ate brisket and baked beans and watermelon and feta salad. Tim brought an incredible almond cake from La Bergamote, and Jonathan made mashed potatoes and raspberry lemonade. We laughed and ate and talked with neighbors we always see coming and going but never sit down with.

One thing we always say: this is our real life. I can't believe this is our real life. This is how we live, in this beautiful place with kind and interesting people.

My heart wells up with gratitude whenever I stop and think about it—the lavish grace that we've been given so much. We had a lovely life for so many years—full of friends and family, work we believed in, a church that meant everything to us. There were moments when it all fell apart that I truly believed goodness was over in our lives, that we'd keep living but would always feel our new lives were a consolation prize, a paler second best, a making do.

I came to believe I didn't deserve goodness anymore, but

after years, after so much therapy, after writing hundreds of thousands of words, tears dripping down my face and neck as I typed, I began to understand, really understand, that I am allowed to heal. I am allowed to be happy. I am allowed to do work I love, to celebrate, to feel joy and delight, to laugh. I'm allowed to invest in my own healing, allowed to protect myself, allowed to tend lovingly to myself in all sorts of ways.

I recently watched workers put up scaffolding on the side of the chapel at the seminary. My little desk in our apartment looks out at the courtyard and the chapel, so I've spent at least a thousand hours admiring the stained glass windows, the red brick. I felt disappointed when I first saw the scaffolding—it's ugly, and the work is loud.

And then all at once, I realized that the scaffolding and the repair work are ways of caring for this building I love. You put up with ugly and loud for a while because you're committed to preserving something of great value. Without the scaffolding and the work, this precious building would crumble and decay.

I feel this truth reverberating through my life, because bricks and glass crumble and crack without that scaffolding from time to time, and human hearts crumble and crack too without deep work and intentional care. We only heal by investing in the difficult and ugly work, even if it isn't pretty, even if it looks like a mess for a while.

Sometimes people equate self-compassion and self-care with being selfish or overly self-focused and believe it's somehow in opposition to faith. But God's fundamental orientation toward us is love. He made us with love, watches over us with love.

Self-compassion isn't unwillingness to take our own failings seriously. It's following God's example, tending to ourselves with the same kindness he shows us, even when we've failed, especially when we've failed. Another way to look at it: self-compassion and self-care are acts of obedience, stewarding well what God has given to us, loving what he loves.

Every one of us was created for love and goodness. And part of my own healing has been recovering that truth about myself. Over time, all the pain—both physical and emotional—started to chip away at me, started to make me believe there was something wrong with me, that I wasn't deserving of goodness or healing or wholeness anymore, that I had done something to bring about all this wreckage.

But that's not true. Pain and loss are a reality of life for all of us, and they're not punishments or referendums on our fundamental worthiness. Life breaks us, and then we put ourselves back together, a little stronger each time, a little braver each time, a little freer each time. And goodness and peace and second chances and joy are not only for the unbroken. They're for all of us. They're for me. And they're for you.

forty-two

Abundance

Our apartment is just like most New York apartments, a mix of lovely and weird and very, very small, but one of the very best things about it is that the kitchen, Aaron's office, and the boys' room face north, onto Twenty-First Street, a beautiful tree-filled street, with a view of the Empire State Building to the northeast. And the living room and our bedroom face south, yielding the loveliest light and also a perfect view of the courtyard. Because we're on the third floor, it feels almost like a tree house—the branches and leaves are the first things we see, then the city buildings behind them and through them.

One thing I've found in all the places we've lived, you always find your space, your little corner, and we all find those spaces for different reasons—for me, it's always, always about the view. For Aaron, it's comfort—the softest, coolest spot. But I'll wedge myself between the oven and the trash can on a tiny barstool for the best light. There's a corner in the kitchen with just enough room for a stool—as long as you don't need to open the oven—and that's where I go first thing in the morning. I open the window and let in the noise—the garbage trucks and honking taxis and yelling children. And I breathe deeply, in and out, and I say thank you.

I used to do a similar thing when we lived in the Midwest

—we had wind chimes that I was crazy about, and when I first came out to the kitchen, before coffee even, I'd open the door to the back porch and swirl the wind chimes. I'd leave the sliding door open until everyone else complained that it was too cold, but I loved it—fresh air, the chimes, a sense of beauty and connection to nature before the day rumbled forward. And now, in one of the busiest cities in the world, it's still the same—straight to the window, the sky, the green lattice of leaves.

The boys are currently entirely enamored with our neighbors —sisters, seventeen and fourteen, while our boys are fourteen and nine. They make an odd foursome, but I remember that age, when the summertime stretches and you're out of your normal routine and you link up with unlikely pals and partners in summer adventures.

The other night, my neighbor Julia asked me to come over a little early before a party to help with dinner prep. She made muhammara and hummus and tzatziki, moussaka and homemade pita. I opened wine bottles and pulled champagne flutes down from the cabinets. I chopped romaine and sliced tomatoes for a Greek salad, set out teacups and small spoons for chocolate mousse.

They just moved into a new apartment, and the windows above the sink are wide and tall, a bright and gorgeous view of the vines on the townhouses across the street, the bell towers of London Terrace, and the Edge and Hudson Yards behind it all.

I was delighted to get her text, because few things in the world bring me as much joy as the hour before a dinner party— plating and chopping, setting timers, setting out glasses and drinks. I love the chaos of it, and the anticipation, the spike in energy.

And then when the party was over, we stayed up way too

late out on the terrace, a clear night with the moon shining like a light, and the next day I couldn't wipe the smile off my face, still floating on the joy of a good party.

There is a sense of abundance in this season—enough time, enough space, enough beauty, enough silence. I'm starting to understand what it means to belong to myself, to recover my own heart, to reassemble all the pieces that have been broken along the way. There are new babies, new families, new adventures. There are songs to write, recipes to try, meals to share, so much to discover and learn and soak up, so much to see and hear and taste, so much to experience on this beautiful planet.

Almost daily, I walk through the practices I've learned along the way—walk, pour it all out, look under the anger, sit with sadness, let go or be dragged, hello to here. Repeat as necessary. And then I push back from my spot at the window. I stretch or write. I do dishes and reach out to friends. I practice forgiveness and practice peace.

In yoga, several poses become a routine—downward dog and cobra and forward fold, taken together, are a sun salutation. This is true in liturgy as well—confession, assurance, Eucharist are three distinct entities, but taken together, there's a movement you're led through, one to the next to the next.

In the kitchen, I light the burner, pull out the cutting board and the knife. I swirl the oil into the pan and begin chopping an onion—you can set up the cutting board and light the stove and chop the onion as entirely separate acts, but there's a rhythm that your body sets when you do them as a set of movements, a dance your fingers know by heart.

And that's how these practices are starting to become for me—a complete movement, a liturgy of sorts, a collection of poses that are more than the sum of their parts.

For whatever reason, it's in the morning when I push myself to face reality. The daytime is when I can wrestle and fight against something, pour out the complicated feelings. Daytime is the space to fight with myself, my dreams, my grief. And it's in the evenings when I need to see what's good, find reasons to express gratitude—I want to close down the day gently, all the raging and wrestling paused until the next day, because nighttime is for rest, for gratitude, for exhaling.

A few weeks ago, at the end of a day, I found myself thinking it had been a lost day—I didn't write or edit, didn't return emails. But here's what I did do—I connected with Aaron, went to therapy, hung out with the kids, tried a new recipe. Maybe what makes a day good or valuable or worthwhile is not what you accomplished, what work you did or thing you fixed or task you checked off a list. Maybe there are other metrics—pleasure, connection, caring for someone, learning something new, experiencing delight. Increasingly, when I think about how to measure a day, a season, a life, I'm committed to different metrics, to abundance instead of scarcity, to care instead of competition, to meaning instead of measuring.

If all you value is work, then productivity is the metric. But if you can shift out from under the weight of that, then the world refracts against itself like a kaleidoscope again, again, again. Not what did you make, but what did you heal from? Not how far did you go, but how hard did you fight to be free?

And you will start to see that time is worth something different, and minutes and hours are ticked out differently—for joy, for play, for another chapter of a book, for setting up for a dinner party with a friend, or for another hour at the table.

forty-three

Keep Going

One of the hazards of being a storyteller is that without even realizing it, you begin to see the narrative arc in every event and unfolding, in every conversation and shift of season. I was absolutely all in for spring this year—spring, spring, spring, like an obsession.

I watched like I was watching an action movie—this is blooming! These branches have buds! Birds are singing, the afternoon light is golden now, unmistakably. I was aching for spring, in all the ways. And spring did come. It came, meteorologically. And the city was increasingly healthy and vaccinated and things were opening up and the energy was electric.

I had expectations for goodness, triumph, healing, redemption. Instead, I was limping, still not sleeping, struggling nearly every day. And my frustration about the expectations only made it worse. This is how it is, even though it isn't how I want it to be. Back to the practices. Consenting to reality. Hello to here.

I wanted a happy ending to this story. I wanted it for me and I wanted it for you. I wanted a happy ending after so many seasons of challenge and change and chaos. I wanted a stretch of ease and answers, a smooth path for a while. I ached for a sense of resolution.

Sometimes it all aligns—spring in the air and inside your

heart, both. But sometimes the warm golden light stuns you with its beauty, like the whole city has been dipped in honey, and your heart is still a block of ice, still winter in every way. That's how this was.

The narrator in me is desperate for resolution, but the plot is still unfolding, as much as I want the story to be over, to catch my breath, to have a still moment to look back over the last few years and decide what they were about. But I don't have a second to decide what it was all about—I'm still in the deep waves, still just trying to gulp some air before the next one hits.

Because I still haven't learned—not after all this pain, not after all this chaos, not after all this loss and heartache and confusion—that we don't control the story as it unfolds. If you want to be in control of a life story, write fiction. Get a doll-house. Puppets maybe.

But our stories, our living-and-breathing, flesh-and-blood, toss-and-turn-all-night, hit-the-snooze-seven-times lives don't ever fit into the formats we've chosen, and I guess I haven't learned that yet—and not for lack of opportunities. This is a stubborn one for me: Life doesn't follow us. We follow it. We run after it, fight against it, catch up to it, make sense of it, get used to it—but it happens to us, not the other way around.

While we all love a before and after, that's not how life is. Most of life is before and after and back to middle and *OMG!* worse than before and tiptoe to middle and then amazing is-this-the-after? We think, *I'm doing it! I'm a star!* And then—another crash. We struggle and learn and forget. We change and change back and change again.

We learn to grab joy and delight when we can. We learn that we don't control plotlines, even though we forget some-times. We learn that every good thing takes time and work and patience. We learn to be suspicious of overnight success or magic solutions. We learn to ask for help, to ask for space, to ask for second chances. We learn how tough we are, and how beloved.

We learn to keep going, because all the times we thought we couldn't take one more step, we did. What's the option? We kept going then, and we can keep going now. It isn't pretty, but if I've learned anything, it's that there's a lot more to life than pretty.

There was a part of my life that about a year ago, I thought I had finally nailed. Thank God. I'd been struggling for about a million years and then I got it. Phew. Finally.

And then it wormed its way back into my life recently, and after a couple months of frustration and struggle and shame and anger, I finally said to Aaron, "Guess what? I guess I haven't learned that yet either. Add it to the list, okay?"

We're strong and we're not. We make progress and then we falter and we show up anyway. We show up anyway, again and again and again, and when we tell the truth about what we're carrying, it makes us feel less alone and less stuck, and when we show up anyway and tell others about what we're carrying, it makes everyone feel less alone and less stuck.

You just do all of it right in the middle of your normal, messy life. The greatest moments of your professional life unfold right while you're having a hard time sleeping or you go back to therapy or you think you might be in early menopause. All we have is right here, right now. Our bodies, our spirits, our fears, the people we love, the people we've failed.

There's no quick fix. There's no overnight success. There's no silver bullet. There's just starting where your feet are, letting yourself be a beginner, showing up anyway, over and over and over. And if that's not as triumphant and motivational as you want it to be, well, okay.

I have a sticky note on my desk on which I wrote, "Keep Going." That's all. Not "Be a Star." Or "Slay All Day." Just keep going. A little every day. A little honesty, a little bravery, a little compassion—for yourself, for everyone else. Keep going, keep going, keep going.

Because I'm playing the long game. We live in a world that loves flashy and fast and fake. But none of that lasts; what lasts is the long game. The legacy. The love that you build day by day. It's about choosing to be present, today and then tomorrow and then the next day. It's about getting up after a fall, over and over.

An old friend came to New York recently, and over ricotta toasts and charred brussels sprouts with pepperoni at a bar on the Lower East Side, she said, "When I met you all those years ago, you were so polished, and you were so capable, and it seemed so natural that your life was so much onstage, with screens and lights and teams and rehearsals and cues. You were so in command of that life—so many people, so many family members, so many big things swirling around you. And now I see you here all these years later, and this is you too. I see you here in this big city, and your life is so much smaller but at the same time so much bigger, and I see you here. This is you too."

And I agree. Who knows what the future looks like? For me or for you, for all of us? I used to think I knew so much, but now all I know is that this rotten, gorgeous world is still the best thing going. God's loving whisper pulses around every corner, and love and goodness still prevail, even when it seems like they don't.

Life will break your heart in a thousand ways, but there's still music and there's still dancing. There's still coffee and toast. There's still kissing and there are still late dinners on busy sidewalks. Twinkly lights, novels, old movies, soft blankets, black-and-white photos, French braids, salty hot french fries dipped in mayo and ketchup.

We're still falling in love. We're still learning to forgive. We're still watching our kids learn and grow and stretch into their next selves. We're still watching the sun as it rises and as it sets, still watching the moon wax and wane. We're still trying, still hoping, still getting it wrong and getting it right.

We're walking together, fighting on sidewalks, making wishes on coins in fountains, praying on our knees. Every generation believes that theirs is special, balancing on an edge, a razor's-edge precipice—now, now, now, all the urgency. But they're gone now, and we will be too, swept up into the past, another special generation on the stage while we watch from the wings. And as we watch them, younger than us but largely the same, we'll see how desperately serious they are about things that don't matter, and how many things they're in danger of missing just the same as we missed them—how often we bickered when we could have been dancing, how many miles we carried our fear like it was the responsible thing to do.

We see now, now that we are older, now that someone else's generation is center stage. We see that we missed so much joy and connection in favor of anxiety and fear, how parched and puckered we lived. When you're old, you realize that most of the things you're worried about are actually going to happen, whether you worry about them or not. Hearts will break and bodies too. People will betray you. Systems will fail. Things you believed were impenetrable will crumble, and looking back all the signs were there, but there's something about us that prefers blindness, especially where love is involved.

Terrible things happen. Treasured things break. If you're

like me, you get tumbled, and the worst of you is on full display. And then you turn back to yourself. You ask for help. You ask for forgiveness. You ask for a second chance. You get up and keep living. More than anything, you forgive yourself.

I hope that the losses of the last several years have made me less blind, less demanding, less entitled. I hope that the pain has stripped from me some of the sense of deserving and imbued in me instead a sense of making peace with what is, a sense of being easily delighted. I hope it takes less and less to bring me joy with each passing month. I hope I am increasingly outraged at injustice in any form, but less offended or horrified when things don't go my way.

Some days I see glimmers of those things—wisdom hard-won, peace hard-earned. I hold tightly to those glimmers like a handful of gold coins, like a treasure. And I let the warmth and weight of those coins in my hand give me the courage to keep going.

I know now that I'm strong enough, brave enough, whole enough to hold it all—how it was and how it ended. What I got wrong, what I made right, who I was, who I wasn't, who I've yet to become. What I miss, what was lost, what's still unfolding. I'm not perfect or shiny or bulletproof. The story of my life is not a fairy tale. It's not a horror story. It's just a story like most stories—dark and light and beautiful and terrible and still being written.

forty-four

Greenport

Today is dark and rainy, rare for summertime. I'm spending a couple days in a fishing village on the North Fork of Long Island, a few hours east of the city. I'm behind on a deadline and need some unbroken alone time. I need to pace in circles around a hotel room without driving anyone crazy.

If I lean, I can see the bay. The sky is low and dark, and the green of the trees is lush. It looks like April or October, nothing summery about it. But that's perfect for my purposes, which are, of course, to stare out the window, type, pace, scribble on the sticky notes and index cards scattered all around the bed.

There's a sense that I'm waiting for a new dream, a new future. It feels weird sometimes, the empty space, but it also feels important, like I'll know when the time comes for what's next, like every day that passes makes me stronger, more able to live in this new world.

I know that four years ago, I never could have imagined living in New York. And now I can't imagine my life without this city, without these sounds and smells and faces. And so I hold on to this when I start fast-forwarding, when I start wanting to know, to be certain, to drill down those roots of security and safety in a new place.

I think of the people I've met and come to love whom I never would have encountered had we never moved. I think about the experiences we've shared—the tears and the laughter, the losses and the adventures.

I'm old enough to realize we don't get everything. We don't get an unlimited number of do-overs or fresh starts. There are some options that do, at some point, close for good. I'm probably never going to be a ballerina or a chef or a cast member on *SNL*—I think those ships have sailed.

But there are still a lot of ships in the harbor, to extend the metaphor. There are a thousand places on this earth my eyes have never seen. There are people who will change my life, somewhere down the road, whom I haven't even met yet. There's work I'll do that I can't even imagine right now.

There's more to learn, more to taste, more to discover. There's more to experience, more to leave behind, more to grasp with both hands.

And I'm going to. I'm going to keep walking, keep loving, keep writing, keep praying. I'm going to keep learning, keep forgiving, keep apologizing, keep moving forward. I'm going to keep inviting, keep listening, keep opening my arms to all of life—terrible and beautiful.

There are meals to savor and faces to fall in love with. There are sunsets to watch like movies and songs to dance to in the kitchen—maybe this kitchen, maybe six kitchens from now—who knows?

I don't. That's for sure. I know less and less and less. But I feel more. I believe more. I trust more deeply in the goodness of our God than I ever have. I'm more aware of the darkness, and more grateful for the light.

I'm walking away, in search of another dream, another adventure, another chance to open my heart, another opportunity to listen and learn and become a wiser, more grounded, more empathetic person than I was a year ago, and a year before that.

I believe there's more out there for all of us. I believe in second chances, in making new lives, in letting go of what's already dead or dying in search of resurrection all around us.

One story doesn't define me. One story doesn't define you. I'm going to write a dozen more at least, and they'll be stories about raising teens and getting older. There will be stories about New York, and wherever life leads after that. About half the things I said I'd never do are now things I've done, so I'm done making predictions.

What I see down the road—possibility, hope, beauty. I don't know any more than that. Loss, I'm sure. Struggle. But I'm not afraid of those things the way I was before. I have a lot more close-up experience with them, and we get through. That's what I know—we get through.

Last night, I sat at the bar of a cozy restaurant in downtown Greenport. It was a rainy, cool night, and I ordered a Manhattan and a lobster roll. I ate slowly, savoring the sweetness of the lobster and the buttery toasted roll. It reminded me how much I like eating out alone, and how rarely I've done it in recent months.

At Christmas this year, we joined via Zoom—the first time in our lives that we weren't with our families for Christmas. My brother-in-law gave out awards to each of the grandchildren, highlighting something they love or love to do. He then gave awards to his parents and his siblings and their spouses—something he respects about them or loves about them. And the award he gave me was the I'm Still Standing Award.

Five years ago, I think I would have found that to be a pretty low bar, sort of a breakeven. You don't get an award for still standing. That's not what I think anymore. I think any of us who weather the raging storms of life and are still standing, still loving, still believing, absolutely deserve an award.

forty-five

One More Song

A couple weeks after school got out, we drove from New York to Illinois to spend a long weekend with Aaron's family. Aaron's sister Emily and her husband, Brad, have a pool and a bonfire pit and Brad put in a par-3 hole, complete with putting green, and for five days we swam and grilled out and made pudgy pies over the fire. I did a lot of French braids for my nieces and sisters-in-law and made sheet pans of nachos and hot Mexican street corn dip, my summer obsession.

On the last night, we let the kids watch a late movie—with cotton candy and popcorn—and then let them join us at the bonfire pit for glow sticks, sparklers, and a night swim. The music was playing and the kids were euphoric and we knew we had to get them to bed at some point, but every time one of the parents said, "Okay, this is it, last song," another parent would start the chant "One more song, one more song." It took forever to get those waterlogged, wound-up kids to bed that night, but it was worth it.

After the family gathering, we stayed a few more days with Aaron's parents, and I'd made plans to see other friends and family I hadn't seen in ages. I sat with my cousins in the backyard on a hot and steamy Sunday night, watching their girls play in the kiddie pool, eating cheese and prosciutto and pickles. We went for a beautiful boat ride on the Fox River with some of our oldest friends, Matt and Casey.

My friend Rachel, the makeup artist, had me and our mutual old friend Brannon over to her house for brunch, and Rachel wanted to show us a few new products she thought we'd like, and just like always, that went from "Let me show you this serum" to "Why don't I just give you a whole fabulous face of makeup?" real fast, and I wasn't complaining at all, although I did feel compelled to explain when I showed up to the next friend's house in full glamour on a Monday afternoon.

Our friend's almost two-year-old daughter, Summer, took Mac out to their chicken coop and showed him how to collect eggs, and they sent us home to my mother-in-law's house with fresh eggs and a nine-year-old scheming how to get a chicken coop in Manhattan.

Just before we left, Summer was in her high chair and I was sitting on a stool next to her, and she turned and put her hands on my cheeks and put her face close to mine, nearly nose to nose. "I love your face!" she said.

One of the things that struck me so deeply was the sense of shared history—the inside jokes, the difficult but necessary questions, the well of knowledge we all share about one another's families and histories, the way I could draw a family tree for any one of those friends, and they could for me.

On my way back to my in-laws' house, I drove past our old house and drove through the church parking lot—something I hadn't done since the last time I was there with my family, more than three years earlier. I drove slowly, soaking it in, absorbing it. I know that building, that parking lot, those walls and floors and ceilings as well as I know my own face in a mirror, and it felt right to bring myself back to it, to breathe it in, to lower my defenses long enough to allow the flood of memories to rush back in, many of them so good, so meaningful.

Something shifted on this visit, the longest stretch of time I had spent in my hometown since moving three years ago. I was able to see my hometown and our church and our old friends and our family as a part of my story, not segmented, not cut off with a hot knife, severed and cauterized. My hometown is my history. Our old church is my history.

I claim it all, include it all, hold it all in my heart. I saw my high school friends and my childhood friends and my cousins. People I've worked with, cried with, raised babies with. And I'm keeping them with me, part of the whole cloth of who I've been and who I'm becoming.

I felt profoundly grateful for the familiarity, for knowing someone across decades, for having the kind of history that allows for a shorthand, shared language, a thousand inside jokes, but even deeper than that, an awareness of one another's hardest days, darkest wounds, scars and secrets.

Something ended on this trip—this terrible winter and spring ended, and summertime came, not a moment too soon. I felt positively bedraggled when we first arrived at my sister-in-law's house, exhausted and dull-skinned, sure that my stress and tiredness showed in my pores and my eyes and my limbs. But the trip itself healed me up a little bit, slowly. Sleep and sunshine, reconnection with so many people I love.

When we left on that last morning, my mother-in-law sent me home with a whole pizza from Lou Malnati's, and in the cooler next to it were blueberries that my aunt Mary picked for us in Michigan and strawberry jam that my cousins made. And all the way back home to New York, I looked down at those three things, and I felt grateful for my hometown, my history, my family and friends, for the flavors and textures and smells and sounds and songs that make a life. Yes, please, one more song.

forty-six

Try Softer

After our summer trip to the Midwest, we arrived back in New York and I knew all my energy had to go into finishing a big work deadline. It was go time, game-face time—all the sports metaphors. And a funny thing happened: for the first time in my life, I couldn't call up that energy. I couldn't command the adrenaline to start firing. I wasn't sad or depressed or checked out, but I was calm and tired, and this was the weird part—I couldn't use my anxiety to spring myself into work and focus. I couldn't, and that had never happened to me before.

I was desperately tired, like close-your-eyes-at-your-desk, sleep-fantasy-level tired. I stared out my window. I lay in bed. I went for a long walk, hoping the physical activity would spark something. I drank copious amounts of caffeine, trying to jump-start my energy. Nothing. If anything, it got worse. I was out of gas, in a deep way, at the very wrong time, and there seemed to be nothing I could do about it.

Before our trip to the Midwest, I'd been working harder than I had in a long time—late nights, early mornings, editing dreams, desk covered with sticky notes. I arrived at my sister-in-law's house absolutely exhausted, and it took me several days to even feel like myself again, longer than usual to recover a sense of buoyancy and spark.

The trip was great, and also, though it yielded such good work inside me, reassembling and restoring important things, the work it required was still work. Even good work is work, and it takes its toll. I was so excited about the forward motion inside me that I failed to consider the emotional miles I was covering, the energy expended.

I was also struggling with long COVID symptoms that were unpredictable and frustrating. Some days, I was fine—normal even. But some days, I was flattened with fatigue, brain fog, and anxiety. Some days, it was hard to draw a full breath, and by the end of the day, I felt like I'd been gasping for air all day, especially on humid days. Insomnia intensified everything, and also I still had almost no sense of smell. My symptoms came and went just often enough for me to wonder if that's what I was really experiencing.

One thing I have learned though—you don't have to know the reason; you just have to trust what's in front of you. Whatever was causing this intense exhaustion didn't really matter. What mattered is that it was real, no matter the root cause.

After several days of trying—and failing—to push through it, I explained it all to my therapist, and he reminded me again that my body and my spirit have a knowing that my mind doesn't have. My mind thinks it's the boss of things, and for many years it was, but so much of my growth over these past years has been about learning to listen to my body and my spirit, to trust them instead of using my mind and my anxiety like a taser, electrifying them to life, pushing my body and my spirit to go and perform and move, no matter what they need or desire. I'm proud of the work I've done, learning to listen, learning to rest, learning to feed myself in truly nourishing ways, learning to tend to my spirit and body in loving ways instead of the harsh ways so many of us were taught along the way.

"It's a sign of health," Andrew reminded me, "that your body and spirit are speaking to you. This is what you've been working toward."

"Yeah," I said, "I get it. But also, bad timing, right? It's go time."

My anxiety in the face of a deadline sent me all the way back to those old ways of living: push, override, game face. The phrase that came to me—the title of Aundi Kolber's wonderful book—was "try softer." I was trying so hard. And hard wasn't working anymore.

And so my therapist looked me straight in the eye and told me to slow everything down. He spoke to me with loving exasperation, because he's been around this block with me a thousand times. "Stop taking hour-long walks in ninety-five-degree heat, okay? Maybe yoga? Breathing? Maybe calm down? Slow everything down instead of trying to jump-start your nervous system by speeding everything up."

He reminded me of Kristin Neff's work on self-compassion, that the research is clear: we do better work—we're actually more productive, not less productive—when we tend to ourselves with kindness and compassion than when we try to motivate ourselves through fear and shame.

These are things I know, these are things I've learned the hard way, over and over, having lived most of my life using fear and shame as weapons I turn on myself. I know better than this. But when anxiety and deadlines come knocking, I forget and it all goes out the window—and I'm back to sports metaphors and brute force.

I did what Andrew told me to do. I got back in bed with a

book of poetry. I rested my body and then made tacos for my family. I know for many people, cooking is the last thing they want to do when they're exhausted, but it's one of those things that always heals me—repetitive motion, connection to senses, making something from nothing. We watched an old movie, all snuggled up, and I went to bed early and slept hard and woke up later than usual.

Little by little, I started to feel like myself again, a gentle energy rising, more like a breeze and less like a leaf blower. I breathed deeply and slowly. I listened to my exhausted body and depleted spirit, and I apologized to both for screaming over them, disregarding their needs, pushing them too hard again.

Henry had a wonderful teacher last year named Donna. She was tough and funny, and when I talked to her on the phone for conferences, she sounded exactly like Fran Lebowitz. She told me all sorts of lovely things about Henry, and then she told me about one of the things they'd been working on together. Henry is one of those kids who will focus with great intensity on whatever he's doing, and sometimes that's good, but sometimes the thing he focuses on doesn't actually require that kind of intensity. Sounds very familiar, of course.

Donna said one of the most important skills you can learn is how to manage your intensity, to dial it down and dial it back up at the right times. The best teachers, she said, are not the ones who arrive at 6:00 a.m. and leave at 6:00 p.m. The best teachers are the ones who go to museums and take art classes and go to the park and throw parties, because when you do all that living, you have something to bring to the classroom. You've learned something about yourself or about the city. You see patterns and metaphors. You have stories to tell and experiences to offer.

I've thought about Donna and her wise words and her gravelly voice a thousand times since that phone call, and every time I feel that old impulse to gut it out, to turn up the intensity, to bend to grind culture, I think about her words and I think about my precious son.

I want Henry to live a spacious, peaceful life, with moments of great focus and moments of great ease. And he'll know how to do that if he sees us do that.

Inhale, exhale, try softer.

forty-seven

Twenty

When Aaron and I were dating, he asked a friend whose marriage he admired, "How do you know if the person you're dating is the person you should marry?"

His friend said, "Is she a grower? Is she a person who's willing to learn, willing to listen, willing to get it wrong but make it right? That's what marriage takes. Marry someone who can and will grow."

Aaron is, categorically, a grower. He's always learning, always asking questions. He's brave enough to admit when he's wrong and to learn how to make it right.

All these years later, I can see with greater and greater clarity how wise that friend's words were: marriage is about a lot of things, but one of the most central is a deep willingness to grow together—toward one another and for one another.

This year, Aaron and I started seeing a couples therapist, and that gave us a safe container to pour out everything we had weathered the last several years. Our therapist gently kept turning us back to one another, back to listening, back to empathy.

At one point, he said, "It sounds to me like your marriage is being reborn." And it is. We celebrated our twentieth anniversary this year, but something new and wobbly-legged is emerging too, like a freshly born deer, exciting and unknown.

TWENTY

This is something I didn't know—that twenty years in, the sight of him out of the corner of my eye could still make my heart leap. That twenty years in, we'd still laugh so much. That twenty years in, we'd find new ways to take care of each other, protect each other, tend to each other's wounds with more and more love and gentleness than we ever knew we could.

I never imagined that the extremely messy man I married twenty years ago would now have a soul mate–level relationship with his vacuum cleaner. I didn't know I'd make a life with a man who wears socks and sandals in public.

I never could have pictured parenting these boys—Henry, broad-shouldered and funny and kind with just exactly my face, and Mac, silly and snuggly and full of swagger with Aaron's eyes and mischief and musicality. Henry's taller than me now and has opinions about fashion and design and film. Mac knows every beat and step of Michael Jackson's choreography and plays a red electric guitar, and it stuns me every day that these two humans living in our apartment were once our tiny babies and are now young men, taller every day, funnier every day, braver every day.

When Aaron and I met and started dating, his little sisters were teenagers. His brother was in junior high. And now they've been a part of my life longer than they haven't, and we've got decades of inside jokes and shared memories. His parents have prayed for us and snuggled our babies. His mom has packed and unpacked my kitchen three times, and his dad has taught our boys how to fish and play the guitar.

Through the turbulence of the last few years, my in-laws didn't miss a beat in terms of their kindness and support for us. They prayed for us, surrounded us with love, reached out on hard days. When so many of the stabilizing parts of my world up to that point were toppling, they were a safe place to land over and over.

A couple years ago, during the hardest stretch of our marriage, we went UpNorth with Aaron's family, like we do every year. I thought about not going, but that would have caused more alarm, I felt. And I love it up there, and I wanted to be there with the kids.

When we arrived at the cabin, one of his sisters and I dragged our chairs down near the ravine in the woods so we could watch our kids while they played. She knew how hard things had been between Aaron and me, and she asked me how it felt to be there with his family.

I told her that, actually, I felt a little nervous. I told her I was sort of afraid they'd all turn on me and throw me in the lake. We laughed, and she put her arm around my shoulder and said, "You're our people. You belong here." And then she said, "Besides, if we're throwing anyone in the lake, let's be honest, it's always going to be Aaron."

When I thought about getting married, one of the only things I wanted was to marry someone with an easy-to-pronounce and easy-to-spell last name. No one gets my first name right, and my maiden name wasn't easy either, and I felt like marriage was my chance to finally get at least one easy name—how about Jones or Smith?

Looking back, the old-fashioned nature of taking a married name strikes me. Twenty years ago, most of our friends took their husbands' names, but not all of them. I did, partially because I knew it meant something to his family and partially because I grew up in a pretty public way and was kind of looking forward to a little lower profile, especially living in our hometown where my family's name was familiar to most people.

Marrying a Niequist, though, did not make my name situation any easier. For the record, it's NEE-kwist, and I'm surprised how many people try to argue with me about it. I just shrug—"Listen, man, I'm not a linguist or a native Swedish speaker, but this is how my in-laws say it, okay?" But also, I'll answer to any name that starts with first name *S* and last name *N*. I did an hour-long interview where they called me Shannon Nelson all the way through because I felt like early on, I missed my window to correct them. At a certain point here at the seminary, they labeled our storage area Aaron and Sharon Niequist . . . I mean, I know Shauna is tricky, but surely you don't think we're Aaron and Sharon, really?

All that to say, what I wanted was an easy name. What I got was a partner who teaches me and challenges me and heals me and walks with me better now than he did twenty years ago, who still dances with me in the kitchen and has really great hair and isn't too proud to learn and relearn with me, to let this old marriage be reborn.

On the night of our twentieth anniversary, we walked down to the West Village, to Via Carota, a gorgeous, cozy Italian restaurant I'd been wanting to go to for years, quite literally. It was about ninety-five degrees, and I made the mistake of wearing heels for the first time since the pre-pandemic days, and I tore up my feet so badly I had to stop and buy a pair of flats at a boutique on Bleecker.

We had arancini and fig and ricotta crostini and the green salad they're famous for, and while we ate, we told stories about our wedding day—funny moments, sweet memories. After dinner, we sat in a park on Hudson for a few minutes and read letters we'd written to each other. They said essentially the same thing. We thanked each other for being willing to keep going, keep changing, keep learning.

Thinking back to that first fundamental question—are they a grower?—we haven't gotten it all right, by any means, but we are growers. They say that the traditional wedding gift for your twentieth anniversary is china, but I think rebirth is an even better gift.

Here's to twenty more, and twenty more after that, NEE-kwist.

forty-eight

Welcome Home

Several years ago, Au Cheval opened in Chicago, a tiny diner with fine dining sensibilities, and people started calling their burger the best in the country. Aaron and I went a handful of times, especially with out-of-town friends or when we were staying in the city for the night.

Their burgers have thin patties and house-made dijonnaise and pickles, and I always order mine with an egg on it, with duck fat fries and garlic aioli, and with an old-fashioned. And every bite is perfect, and that's why people—including us—put up with outrageously long wait times.

I had heard that they opened an Au Cheval in Tribeca at the end of an alley but hadn't had a chance to go pre-pandemic, and then it closed, along with so many other restaurants, and it wasn't clear if it would reopen.

On a cool, cloudy Saturday, I realized I needed to get out of the apartment, out of the seminary, out of our neighborhood. I was writing on a deadline, and in order to get that work done, I had to make my world pretty small for a while—no meetings, no socializing, working long days, taking short breaks to walk around the seminary and then back to my desk. All that was good, but by the end of the week, I needed a change of scenery.

Our friends Michael and Kyndi were up for dinner, and

they left it up to me to find a spot. I scrolled through various apps for reservations, started making a list of options, and then I saw an early slot for Au Cheval, and without even checking with anyone, I booked it.

Our friends had never heard of it, and I was a little nervous that it wasn't open after all, that the reservation app was wrong. No one answered the phone when I called, and the map on my phone still categorized it as temporarily closed. We rode bikes down the West Side Highway, cutting in at Canal. When we rounded the corner, the space looked dark, and it looked like the metal gates were down over the windows.

When I tried the door, at first it didn't open, but then it swung open as a man was leaving, and all of a sudden we were in a bustling dining room with high ceilings and palpable energy, and I was a little giddy giving the hostess my name—maybe it was a really long couple weeks, or riding a Citi Bike on Canal Street, or the fear that I was leading our party on a wild-goose chase, or the unexpected news that the restaurant had reopened without my knowing. All of it, probably. I was delighted.

We had great salads and fries and cocktails, and before the burger came, I hadn't anticipated having such a strong sense of taste memory—especially because post-COVID, I still have almost no sense of smell, and my sense of taste is still a little bit off.

But that first bite of smoky charred beef and cheese and runny egg and dijonnaise absolutely floored me. It was delicious, and more than that, it was deeply familiar, transporting me immediately to a place and a time and a self I used to be. I was flooded with memories of our life in Chicago, dates Aaron and I had been on, friends I'd sat with as we ate these same burgers all those years ago. All very Proustian, of course, and it's fitting that a Chicago burger with a runny egg would be my madeleine.

I'm a big believer in sense memory, and specifically taste memory—that's part of why I'm such a fan of repertoire cooking—having a handful of things you always make when people come over because that hit of familiarity, of taste memory, is so important, especially as we emerge from such a deeply disconnected, chaotic, isolated season. We're so desperate to travel back to other places and other times through flavor and smell because we're longing for so many things we lost—holidays we didn't spend together, vacations we didn't get to take, beloved food traditions we missed, or restaurants we didn't get to visit the last couple years.

Taste memory is often nostalgic and often simple—very few of us cling to memories of sophisticated, fussy food. Our food nostalgia is more often homey, comforting flavors—pans of pasta that remind us of Italian grandmothers, cookies that take us back to childhood, the smell of charcoal that brings us back to summertimes gone by.

I felt like that first bite of the burger drew a map inside my chest—the exact route to that tiny restaurant on Randolph Street in Chicago. It flooded me with memories of who we were in that season, what was the same and what was different. And it made me reflect on what I do miss, and what I don't.

More than anything, of course, I miss people—I miss my cousins and my sisters-in-law. I miss my friends from high school. And I miss that sense of rootedness and familiarity, that even if I don't know someone, we could probably find between us a mutual friend.

When people in New York hear we're from the Chicago area,

they often say something like, "Oh, so you get it." And we always correct them, letting them know that we lived in the suburbs of Chicago, not the city, and also that the two cities are fundamentally, categorically different. I get why people think they're similar at first glance—big cities, similar climates.

In my experience, though, that's where the similarities end. To me, the deep Midwesternness of Chicago undergirds everything—it's warmer and friendlier than New York, and it's more connected to the surrounding area, to the rural areas and lakes and college towns, whereas New York City, at least in our experience, is more a world unto itself, truly global but holding the surrounding area almost at arm's length.

But no matter the differences, I was submerged in memories of another place, another time, another self, in just that one bite, in just exactly the same way a song can take you to another continent or the scent of a perfume can take you back thirty years to your first date. Still today I'm feeling within my chest the ache of loving a place from a distance.

One of my first really visceral moments of missing Chicago was our first Mets game. Our friends Annette and Andrew and their kids were visiting from California, and it was such a fun night, but at the same time, I was so thrown off by being at a baseball game that wasn't at Wrigley Field. Everything felt just a couple degrees off from normal—wrong colors of uniforms, wrong smells and flavors, wrong traditions. Close enough to ring some memory bell in my chest, but decidedly not the same.

In our last couple years in Chicago, especially as things became more complicated in our lives, Wrigley Field was a bright spot, a safe zone, a place we came back to again and again. I remember each of the boys' first night games—how excited they were, but also how heavy their eyes were by the later innings.

Over the years, I'd scoped out every inch of Wrigley, knowing where they sold the Bob Chinn's mai tais and the ice cream in the little helmets. We knew the usher in the section where we usually sat and where to park, and going to Cubs games felt like a fixed point in our chaotic world. And so that first night at Citi Field, we were having fun, but I was also feeling that deep disorientation—this isn't our stadium. This isn't our home.

I haven't felt that very often since we've been here, I think because the worlds feel so different to me, because to me you couldn't mistake our old life for our new life if you tried. The briny, salty smell of the ocean here is so different from the sweetish, mineral smell of the Great Lakes. The accents are giveaways every time, and even the vocabulary. Sometimes I can hear a little New York in our kids' voices, when they say "sure" or "tourist" or "orange." People dress differently here than they do in the Midwest, especially women, and New Yorkers hold to totally different food traditions—strong feelings about bagels and dumplings and oysters abound.

Everyone has their own math of what makes someone a New Yorker—some people say it's ten years or seven. Some say it's weathering a disaster—9/11 or Hurricane Sandy or the pandemic. Others say it's when you find yourself fighting with your significant other at full volume on the sidewalk or when you slap your palm down on the hood of a cab for ignoring the pedestrian right-of-way.

I don't know exactly what it is, but I do know that Aaron and I both hit significant milestones this week. He cut across several lanes of traffic *and* bulldozed some traffic cones to get to the correct lane to enter the Lincoln Tunnel. And last night, when our smoke alarm battery started beeping at 10:00 p.m., I threw on a sweater over my floral nightgown and walked to Rite Aid for a replacement, and no one looked twice at me.

Just after we moved, one of the leads in *Wicked* invited us to see one of her last performances and meet her backstage. She was kind and funny and super talented, and the boys' eyes were like dinner plates as they got to walk out onto the stage at the Gershwin Theatre after the show. As we left, she gave us a signed photo that was personalized to our family. "Welcome home," it read.

I asked a friend about it, and he told me that's a thing people say here: "Welcome home." No matter where you're coming from, no matter how long you'll stay—welcome home.

A few years later, here I am, realizing home isn't singular, that you don't lose one, but rather your world and your heart expand with each new home and new set of experiences, each new self and new street. The old ones stay, precious and tender, unlocked occasionally by a bite or a moment. And the new ones make your heart bigger and bigger, and your world bigger and bigger.

New York is my home. And Chicago is my home. And Aaron is my home. And more than anything, I've learned the hard way what it means to come home to myself, deeper than a city, deeper than a circle of relationships or shared history, deeper even than a family or a partner. Underneath all the other layers of identity and belonging, beneath all the attachments and expectations, all the longing and unbelonging, all the chaos and loss and change, I found my own self, my own home.

forty-nine

Next Self

Earlier this month, just at that distinct razor's-edge turn from summer to fall, we had one of those days when it rained absolutely all day, rain on the rooftops as we woke up, rain on the rooftops as we went to sleep. That day, I was working at a workspace down in the Meatpacking District, six blocks from our apartment, and I was late to meet a friend there, so I threw on a pink dress and checkered Vans and ran out the door. We worked for a few hours, walked to Chelsea Market for banh mi, worked some more, and then in the early evening, I walked home just as the rain was tapering off for a few hours but the skies were still dark and low.

There's a lot of talk about invisibility—who we notice, who we don't—and certainly I've noticed at different moments in my life what people see and what they don't. When I was younger and thinner and blonder, I noticed eyes flicking up and down over my body. When I've been heavier and as I get older, sometimes I become something like a piece of furniture, something the eye skips over. My regular walking buddy is a striking former model, and people regularly bump into me because they're checking her out, and as I've mentioned before, this is not my greatest season in terms of my relationship to my body or how it looks reflected back to me in the mirror.

Then recently, I took the plunge and cut my hair short for the first time in more than twenty years, cutting off all the golden-blonde pieces to leave just the natural darker tones and the abundance of gray that I discovered in the pandemic months. This was my gutsy cut, my brave I-just-turned-forty-five cut, and one way to explain it is that I believed in it but didn't quite like it yet—I didn't feel like myself, and if I'm honest, maybe I was realizing some ways I'd been clinging to all that goes with long blonde hair, and maybe I was also feeling the lack of it.

So it's dark and rainy, and I'm running down Tenth Avenue and back throughout the course of the day, from the workspace to Chelsea Market and back. I'm deep into my invisibility phase, and I barely recognize my own self with this short, silvery brown hair. But I'm wearing a nearly floor-length tiered hot-pink dress, nothing subtle about it, swirling around my ankles as I cross intersections and avoid puddles.

And by the end of the day, I lost count of how many people talked to me about that dress. An old man stepped aside with a gallant gesture on the sidewalk, as if to say, *Come through, my lady.* One woman shouted to me from a bike all the way across the intersection, "You are rocking that pink dress, lady!"

Young people and old people, men and women, all talked to me about this ridiculously pink dress. I was simultaneously deeply uncomfortable and oddly energized. I was so deep into both chosen and experienced invisibility by that point. I didn't feel seen and I desperately didn't want to be seen, and the only reason, honestly, that I wore that pink dress was because I was running late and almost nothing in my closet fit well and the usual navy and black-and-white staple dresses were at the dry cleaner. The last thing I was trying to do was swan down the sidewalk like a human ice cream cone. The last thing I wanted to do was be seen.

But I was. I was seen, and apparently that vibrant color made people happy, the way flowers make people happy and outrageous hats make people happy, and it made me think about how important it is to contribute to joy, even when—especially when—it takes a little bravery to do it.

It seems that in some small way that silly dress brought a moment of lightness to my neighbors, and that's worth something. It made me think about all the years I kept myself hidden, camouflaged, in neutral colors and the most boring possible things in order to not draw attention to a body I don't approve of. But what if another phenomenon is unfolding entirely? What if my willingness to be seen, just as I am, with my kooky new hair and my flamingo-colored dress, isn't about me, but it's a freedom and a lightness I offer to the people around me? Here's something that will make you smile—not my own beauty, certainly, not my body or my face or my hair, but my willingness to show up in full color, in full bloom, one bright spot on a dark day.

This seems to be at the heart of everything right now—a willingness to show up, unarmed and unfiltered and wildly imperfect, looking the reality of life full in the face. Willingness to show up, not out of a place of strength, but out of a shared vulnerability. *Here we are. Here's what's been broken along the way. Here are our bruises and scars, our fears and secrets. Here I am, showing up anyway.*

As the weather begins to slouch toward autumn, my memories of our life this time last year are flooding back, more each day. We were largely so alone, all of us. Working from home, attending school on a screen. The world was quiet and terrifying. Somewhere along the way, we developed a little Friday night routine, the handful of families that were a part of our quarantine pod. Looking back, I don't know why we didn't have dinner together every night, why we weren't sprawled all over each other's couches all day, lamenting the world and our lives, but we weren't. We soldiered through the workweek and the school week, and then we gathered on Friday night to watch the new Marvel show. Kyndi made popcorn with candy that the kids could mix in and Michael made Manhattans, and we watched a show. And then we danced. We danced along with the Just Dance app, song after song. There were group favorites and requests we begged for every week. There were ones we nailed and ones we were terrible at, and in those dark, cold, isolated months, I don't know if anything else brought me more joy than those nights of popcorn and dancing.

And also, what I remember is that the months and months of isolation made it hard to show up, hard to connect—inertia and fear and exhaustion told us to just stay home, just stay isolated. It felt like I had forgotten how to talk to people. I definitely forgot how to dress and still haven't resumed anything like a makeup regimen. Every time we walked over to Kyndi and Michael's apartment, it felt like getting off a long flight, blinking and flinching. *Where are we? What just happened to us?*

But we showed up, and we danced. We danced and danced like wild, crazy people, parents mortifying kids, wiggling and sashaying wildly, jumping and booty shaking.

There's so much I don't know about this next season, about the world or about my own life or my own next self, but here's what I know: there will be dancing.

There will be pink dresses. There will be play. And delight and beauty and hope. And I'll keep showing up in my ridiculous pink dress, despite my longing for invisibility. Because who knows who it is on the sidewalk who desperately needs an infusion of whimsy or enchantment or joy. Sometimes it's me, and sometimes it's that sweet old man across from me on the sidewalk, and as long as we all keep showing up, keep dancing, keep seeing each other, I think we'll all get to wherever we're going, and I think we'll all discover our wild, weird, brave next selves along the way.

fifty

Still Yes

Several years ago—what actually seems like a lifetime ago—I got a tattoo on the tender inside of each forearm. On my left arm, a red heart, a reminder that for the rest of my life, anything I make, write, create, build, I want to come from a place of love—not competition or fear or ambition or proving, only love.

And on my right arm, in navy ink, in my friend Lindsay's lovely script, the word *yes*. In order to rebuild a life that matched my values, for a long time, I had to say a lot of hard noes—I had to learn to disappoint people, and I had to make my life, especially my work life, much smaller and slower. I wanted to be a person of meaning, connection, depth, creativity, but for all sorts of reasons, I bought into hustle culture, and my life became increasingly marked by exhaustion and isolation. I wasn't the partner I wanted to be. I wasn't the parent I wanted to be. And so I learned the hard way how to remake a life from the inside out, and it mostly involved saying no over and over.

It was the right thing, the only thing, but at the same time, I needed to remind myself that all those noes were in service of a bigger yes—yes to love and play and my kids and my marriage. Yes to adventure and grace and rest and delight. Yes to wild and silly and weird and delicious. The tattoo, then, was a promise to myself, a reminder. *This is who you are. You are yes*

—openhearted, not closed off, willing to taste the entire world, to revel in every inch of it.

I grew up on sailboats in a family of sailors, surrounded by all manner of nautical accoutrements. And like anything you're surrounded by, over time it becomes familiar and you fail to wonder about it. But I read something recently about nautical flags—the kind that are, frankly, everywhere in our life at the lake—at the yacht club, in the boat barn, these sort of ubiquitous colorful flags that are as familiar to a sailing family as anchors and stripes. There's a flag that means *yes*. And that *same* flag is the one used in a regatta to tell the sailors that the racecourse has been changed. Yes, and also—the path you planned has now been altered.

Oh, I feel that in my soul. Yes, and change course. Yes, and the future is different than you anticipated. Keep going, but keep in mind that all your plans and preparations just went out the window.

It reminds me of the improv rule "yes, and . . ." We want "yes, period," right? We're okay with moving forward, as long as we get to control what's coming next. But that's not how it works. Not in improv, not on the water, not in life. Yes, and. Yes, and change course. Yes, into the unknown. Yes, even though everything's different. Still yes. Sometimes when I'm scared or I feel myself closing in on myself, self-protective and hunched, I look down at that yes. I roll my shoulders back down and take a deep breath and I say yes to whatever is scary or hard or complicated in front of me. I say yes. Yes is who I am. Still yes.

I still say yes to life. I still say yes to creative work, to the church gathered, to storytelling and hospitality and living with an open heart. I still say yes to risk, to adventure, to diving into the wreck, to making something beautiful from loss.

STILL YES

I still believe in Jesus Christ, in the power of the table—both the Eucharist and also takeout around a cramped apartment table. I still believe in forgiveness, laughter, pizza for breakfast, dancing in the kitchen. I still say yes to second chances, staying out too late, watching the sunset like a movie, holding hands, farmers markets, taking the long way home.

> Is the world still beautiful? Still yes.
> Do our stories still matter? Still yes.
> Am I still hopeful? Still yes.

> Will I trust people?
> Will I trust God?
> Will I trust myself?

> *Still yes, yes, yes.*

Acknowledgments

This book, more than any other I've written, was a team effort. Carolyn McCready, Angela Scheff, and Chris Ferebee talked me off a thousand ledges, made every page of this book better, and kept me company even—especially—on the hardest stretches of this journey.

So much love and gratitude to Michael and Kyndi, David and Kate, Michael and Julia, Jonathan, and Tim, aka The Close: thank you for happy hours and dance parties and movie nights and funny memes and for being our home team in one million little and big ways. Thank you as well to Jennifer and Alexander, and to my treasured neighbor JRW, for showing me the NYC ropes. Thanks to Andrew, my therapist and friend, for helping bring me back to life and back to myself. Many thanks to treasured friends who walk with me so well, even across the distance, especially Annette, Kristi, Jon, and Emily G.

All my love to our extended families: we adore you and we treasure our time together, never more so than after a long-distance move and a global pandemic. Here's to fewer Zooms and more hugs in coming months and years.

Thank you times one thousand to Henry and Mac, two of my favorite people on earth: thank you for teaching me how to be brave and creative every day, for making me laugh, and for always being willing to try a new diner or bookstore with me.

And of course, always, to Aaron: I never would have become a writer if it wasn't for your encouragement. And I would have quit after every book if it wasn't for your encouragement. And I threatened to throw my laptop in the Hudson River a dozen times while trying to finish this book, but I never did . . . because of your encouragement. Thank you for believing in me more than I've ever believed in myself. Here's to twenty more years. I love you.

Present Over Perfect

Leaving Behind Frantic for a Simpler, More Soulful Way of Living

Shauna Niequist

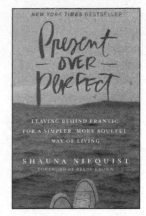

New York Times bestselling author Shauna Niequist invites you to consider the landscape of your own life and what it might look like to leave behind the pressure to be perfect and begin the life-changing practice of simply being present—in the middle of the mess and the ordinariness of life.

As she puts it, "A few years ago, I found myself exhausted and isolated, my soul and body sick. I was tired of being tired, burned out on busy. And it seemed almost everyone I talked with was in the same boat: longing for connection, meaning, depth, but settling for busy. I am a wife, mother, daughter, sister, friend, neighbor, writer, and I know all too well that settling feeling. But over the course of the last few years, I've learned a way to live, marked by grace, love, rest, and play. And it's changing everything. *Present Over Perfect* is an invitation to this journey that changed my life. I'll walk this path with you, a path away from frantic pushing and proving, and toward your essential self, the one you were created to be before you began proving and earning for your worth."

Shauna offers an honest account of what led her to begin this journey and a compelling vision for an entirely new way to live: soaked in grace, rest, silence, simplicity, prayer, and connection with the people who matter most to us.

Available in stores and online!

Bread & Wine

A Love Letter to Life Around the Table *with Recipes*

Shauna Niequist

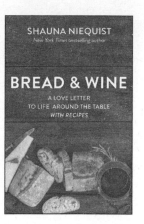

Bread & Wine is a literary feast about the moments and meals that bring us together.

New York Times bestselling author Shauna Niequist offers an enchanting mix of funny and vulnerable storytelling in this collection of recipes and essays about the surprising and sacred things that happen when people gather around the table.

With beautiful and evocative writing, Shauna explores the sweet and savory moments when family and friends sit down together. She invites us to see how God teaches and feeds us, even as we nourish the people around us, and ponders how hunger, loneliness, and restlessness lead us back to the table again.

Part cookbook and part spiritual memoir, *Bread & Wine* illuminates how sharing food together mirrors the way we share our hearts with each other, and with God. And it explores what it means to follow a God who reveals his presence in breaking bread and passing a cup.

For anyone who has found themselves swapping stories over plates of pasta, sharing take-out on the couch, laughing over a burnt recipe, and lingering a little longer for one more bite... this book is for you.

Recreate the meals that come to life in each essay with recipes for Goat Cheese Biscuits, Bacon-Wrapped Dates, Mango Chicken Curry, Dark Chocolate Sea Salt Toffee, and many other wonderful dishes. A satisfying read for heart and body, this book is one you'll want to keep close at hand all year round.

Available in stores and online!

Bittersweet

Thoughts on Change, Grace, and Learning the Hard Way

Shauna Niequist

"The idea of *bittersweet* is changing the way I live, unraveling and reweaving the way I understand life. Bittersweet is the idea that in all things there is both something broken and something beautiful, that there is a sliver of lightness on even the darkest of nights, a shadow of hope in every heartbreak, and that rejoicing is no less rich when it contains a splinter of sadness.

"It's the practice of believing that we really do need both the bitter and the sweet, and that a life of nothing but sweetness rots both your teeth and your soul. Bitter is what makes us strong, what forces us to push through, what helps us earn the lines on our faces and the calluses on our hands. Sweet is nice enough, but bittersweet is beautiful, nuanced, full of depth and complexity. Bittersweet is courageous, gutsy, audacious, earthy."

Niequist, a keen observer of life with a lyrical voice, writes with the characteristic warmth and honesty of a dear friend: always engaging, sometimes challenging, but always with a kind heart. You will find *Bittersweet* savory reading, indeed.

"This is the work I'm doing now, and the work I invite you into: when life is sweet, say thank you and celebrate. And when life is bitter, say thank you and grow."

Available in stores and online!

Cold Tangerines

Celebrating the Extraordinary Nature of Everyday Life

Shauna Niequist

Cold Tangerines is a collection of stories that celebrate the extraordinary moments hidden in your everyday life. It is about God, and about life, and about the thousands of daily ways in which an awareness of God changes and infuses everything. It is about spiritual life and about all the things that are called nonspiritual life that might be spiritual after all. It is the snapshots of a young woman making peace with herself and trying to craft a life that captures the energy and exuberance we all long for in the midst of the fear and regret and envy we all carry with us. It is both a voice of challenge and song of comfort, calling you upward to the best possible life, and giving you room to breathe, to rest, to break down, and break through.

   Cold Tangerines offers bright and varied glimpses of hope and redemption, in and among the heartbreak and boredom and broken glass.

Available in stores and online!